Table of Contents

Foreword to the Revised Edition

In April 2011, in a cramped and horribly overpriced hotel room in London, I began the outline for a dating advice book.

For anyone who has tried to write a book, they know that starting it is the most daunting part. There were so many considerations, so many ideas, so many goals and ambitions. And for a few days, I was paralyzed with all of the potential.

But I soon decided to limit myself to one specific aim. I asked myself, "What book do I wish I would have read when I was single and struggling in my dating life? If I had only read one book, what do I wish it had told me?"

As the weeks went by, it turned out that I wished it had told me a lot. The book spilled out of me in a somewhat involuntary manner, a kind of intellectual vomit. I was touring Europe, giving talks and coaching live at the time, and I would often finish up a session with a client or do a Q&A with a small audience and immediately run to my hotel room to jot some of the ideas that had spewed out of my mouth into the now ballooning book.

I also decided early on that I wanted to make the book different stylistically. I had read pretty much every other dating advice book on the market and thought most of them were garbage. I already knew the core ideas of this book were going to be different – deeper, more personal, more emotional. But I also wanted the style of the book to be different. Perhaps I was up my own ass with self-importance, but I wanted to give it a bit more of a literary flair. I wanted the beauty and joy of the dating experience to come across in the writing itself. I didn't just want to lay out step-by-step plans and information to be memorized, I wanted to move the reader, since after all, the whole point of the book is that dating and romance is about just that: allowing yourself to be moved, both emotionally and physically.

I wrote the book in less than three months. Most of it was written in hotel rooms and small apartments across Europe: first London, then Bristol, then Prague, then St. Petersburg, and it was finally finished in Budapest.

The first version of the book was long and sloppy: 366 pages, with at least that many typos, grammatical errors, and dumb tangents. At the time, my aspirations were fairly pedestrian. I wanted to be able to make some money online without having to physically be in one spot, as almost four years of constant travel to do the coaching thing was wearing on me.

But I also wanted to get my ideas out into the world and hopefully make a dent in the dating advice industry since, at the time, I felt that what I had to say was quite different from the vast majority of toxic "Pick Up" advice that was being taught to men.

The book came out on July 5th, 2011. It was self-published through Amazon and my own website. That first month it only sold a few hundred copies – mostly blog readers and former clients of mine. Many of them reported to me many of the mistakes and helped me edit it over the proceeding weeks and a few small updates were released soon after. By the fall of that year, I felt good that it was out there and people liked it and soon moved on to other projects.

But as the months rolled on, the book began to take on a life of its own. With no marketing, no publicity, no promotion, and a shitty cover I made myself in Photoshop, the book's sales grew exponentially each month. Like a mind virus, infecting people's brains so that they could move on and infect others, men began recommending it to their friends, and then *their* friends recommended it to their friends, and soon their friends' friends were buying it for their brothers and cousins and even newly divorced fathers and uncles. It was soon being recommended on websites and forums so much that I began to get emails asking me to stop spamming. But I wasn't spamming. I wasn't doing anything. It was simply the readers.

By early 2012, to my pleasant surprise, I was earning enough to make a living as an author. So I quit coaching and focused solely on my writing. That same summer I also gave the book its first real revision. I hired a designer to create a real cover. I chopped about 50 of the more pedantic and excessive pages. I simplified some of the terms and theories and tried to make them more reader-friendly. What I consider the first 'professional' version of *Models* was released in August of 2012.

From there the book went on to become the highest selling men's dating advice book for years at a time, outselling mainstays such as Neil Strauss's *The Game* and Erik Von Markovik's *The Mystery Method*, often even outselling most women's dating advice books, which is kind of unheard of in the industry. It was a perennial bestseller in the category on Amazon and has actually reached a point where many popular men's dating advice forums and sites list it with a "read this before asking any questions" note in their FAQs or sidebars.

By 2013, I felt as though I was finished with the book. I was ready to move on. I was preparing to relaunch my site and start writing articles for both genders with topics ranging from personal psychology to the cultural effects of smartphones and newsfeeds. I was leaving dating advice behind for good.

Over the next two years, my site's popularity exploded. Over 20 million people read it in 2015 alone. Yet *Models* has always persisted, always there in the background. Always a throbbing reminder of where I came from, as well as the virtue of taking a calculated risk and seeing where it led me.

Because, most people don't realize this now, but *Models* was a huge risk when it came out.

See, back in 2011, few pieces of dating or relationship advice talked about blunt honesty, about accepting rejection or even polarizing people for negative responses. Vulnerability was considered a vulgar word among most men and anything that didn't get you laid as soon as possible was often deemed pointless, or even worse, being "beta."

And, *god forbid*, you talk about emotions or trauma or feelings of inadequacy. Like really, who the fuck wants to hear about that, you pussy? Go approach more!

But I had known from working with hundreds of men around the world that most of their dating problems had little to do with "knowing what to say" or tactics to get women to sleep with them sooner. The vast majority of these men's problems were emotional. They were rooted in deep inabilities to experience intimacy. They were born out of an irrationally negative self-perception that came from a lifetime of feeling inferior and inadequate around women. They came from men who were scared to look reality in the eye and still smile.

I knew when I put these pages together that they were either going to revamp much of the industry or they were going to be laughed off the Amazon sales page and I'd soon go get a day job.

But today, I'm happy to say that much of the men's dating advice industry has followed suit and is now extolling the virtues of honest expression, of finding courage and confidence through vulnerability, and investing oneself into becoming a better man rather than simply appearing as though you're a better man.

Sometimes I get emails from readers who send me videos or passages from other dating advice companies or coaches, who five years ago were the king of the douches, who used to wear ridiculous outfits and give "advice" such as whipping out your cock in public and screaming nonsense at women. Now, many of these men are preaching the virtues of living honestly and respecting women's desires as well as your own. Often the reader will ask me, "This guy is ripping you off, does this piss you off?" And actually, it doesn't. It makes me happy and proud.

I was born in Texas and we have a tendency to prattle on about ourselves (if you imagine me sitting on a porch sipping a can of cheap beer with a shotgun strewn across my lap, that's about how writing all of this feels), so let me cut to the chase here and answer what you're probably wondering, "What the hell is with the latest revision and why did you do it?"

This latest revision comes on the tail end of finishing a new book to be published in 2016. Upon completing that book, I looked back through *Models* and once again felt that it was in need of an update, particularly in the writing department. I still feel good about the core ideas and advice of the book. But in the four years since I last touched it, my writing has improved by leaps and bounds and my explicative abilities have grown. So, once again, I combed through the text: concepts were clarified, advice was reworded to be more precise, and excessive nonsense was trimmed or removed entirely. This version of *Models* that you are reading right now is the clearest, most concise, and therefore, likely the most powerful version to date. I'm confident in that.

For older readers, changes include:

- Removing most of Chapter 1 and moving some sections to other parts of the book.

- Changing 'True Confidence' back to 'non-neediness' (the original term from the first version). I put 'True Confidence' in the second version of the book because I thought that it was more digestible to the average reader. In hindsight, I think it's just a vague and "feel good" term. I always liked (and most readers still prefer) the original term that I totally made up out of thin air: non-neediness. This term has been re-instated along with added explanation of where it came from.
- Changing 'False Confidence' to narcissism. Narcissism is a new term entirely for the book and one that I think is more precise and comprehensible. Although I do think 'False Confidence' is a pretty accurate description of narcissism in most cases.
- Being more explicit about the ideas of consent, recognizing and responding to how women feel, and basically treating them like people and not objects. This was always implied in earlier versions of the book, but after being horrified at some of the emails I get from men and how they interpret the book, I've decided to be more explicit about this. This is a book about people speaking and relating to other people, not obtaining objects or status symbols.
- Cleaned up a lot of the writing. Made some sections less dry. Added a bit more humor.
- Deleted about 30 pages of unnecessary tangential stuff, repetitive explanations, and just long, rambly writing in places.

If you're new to the book, don't worry about the changes, just dive right into it. If you're an older reader, then the first few chapters and the last few are the ones with the most added/changed, while Chapter 8 (formerly 9) is the one with the most removed.

In the end, although existing in a genre that's considered by most to be a joke, I'm incredibly proud of this book. Not only did it birth me a career doing what I love, but I feel as though it took my wildest aspirations when I wrote it and surpassed them with ease. Most books die off after a couple years, but *Models* continues to chug along, as resilient and polarizing and vulnerable as ever, changing the lives of men in its wake.

Or at least, that's what I like to tell myself.

And for most of that success, I have nobody to thank but you: the returning readers, the people who read the book and shared it with their friends or recommended it on websites, the people who bought five copies and gave it to their friends and family members. Without your enthusiasm and support for the ideas here, especially early on, they would likely have been lost to the cesspool of failed self-published books on Amazon. So to you, thank you.

Mark Manson

December 28th, 2015

A Quick Note to Female and LGBT Readers

The popularity of *Models* has brought it to the attention of a number of people that the book was not originally conceptualized and written for. A number of single women, as well as gay, lesbian, bi, and trans people have emailed me over the years asking if the book's concepts apply to them.

At first, this surprised me. And then what surprised me more is that as I went through the concepts in the book, I realized that the answer was a resounding 'yes,' these concepts apply to everyone. Although there are a few caveats.

The core principles of the book – Non-Neediness (Chapter 1), Vulnerability (Chapters 2-3), Unconditionality (Chapter 3), Polarization and Rejection (Chapters 4-6), Demographics (Chapter 7), Overcoming Shame and Anxiety (Chapters 9-10), and Intentions (Chapter 11) – apply to all human beings, regardless of gender, orientation, genitalia or whatever.

The parts of the book that won't directly apply are a number of the specific examples and implementations of these core principles. For example, in most cultures, men are expected to initiate in almost every phase of courtship, therefore, the anxieties they face (Chapters 9-10), the challenges with vulnerability they will confront (Chapter 3) and so on, will look a little bit different than they would for a hetero woman or someone of another orientation.

As long as you keep this in mind as you move throughout the book and attempt to apply the core principles to your own dating situation, you should be fine. Women, like men, must polarize. Gay men must work on their neediness and vulnerability as well. Lesbians must learn to look at the intentions behind their communication rather than communication itself. But because the book was initially written for a hetero male audience, the examples and specific pieces of advice given are for their situations.

A number of female readers have requested that I write a female version of *Models* and that is something I might do one day. But in the meantime, this is all we've got.

As a final note, the only Chapters that I feel are primarily written for the hetero male situation are Chapters 8 and 14. Other readers will find these chapters the least relevant. The Introduction (which begins on the next page) is also largely oriented towards hetero men and discusses modern-day masculinity. So feel free to skip it and go straight to Chapter 1.

Introduction: Movement

In our post-industrial, post-feminist world, it's not as clear as it used to be what a man is or what he should be. Centuries ago, a man's duty was power and protection. Decades ago, it was to work and provide. But now? We're not quite sure. We are either the first or second generation of men to grow up without a clear definition of what our social roles are supposed to be and without a model of what it is to be strong and attractive men.

This book's goal is to provide that model, to provide a model of what being an attractive man of integrity and maturity looks like in the 21st century. That means going past the standards of protector and provider, of strength and stoicism, and improving ourselves into something bigger and better, something more admirable and desirable.

Ten years ago, when I first began helping men improve their relationships with women, I had no idea the rabbit hole of information and self-improvement I was about to go down, both for myself and for others. At the time, the primary concerns in my dating life revolved around which drink specials were going on that Thursday night and which one of the five Jennas in my phone was the one I met last weekend.

It wasn't until I sat down and tried to get *other men* to the point where they had five Jennas in their phone that I had a glimpse of the profundity and underdevelopment of most men's emotional and sexual world and how difficult it is to inspire a genuine movement within them to open up that world.

I won't lie, in hindsight, getting *myself* to that point seems easy now by comparison. Growing up, I had always been somewhat of an average guy, although I had little luck with the ladies.

Then in 2005, after being cheated on and left by my first love, I was emotionally distraught and slightly traumatized. I became obsessive. A desperate need for validation and affection from women arose within me and I spent an inordinate amount of time pursuing that validation and affection, far more than most men ever do. I overcompensated and soon became driven to sleep with every girl in the Boston area who would let me anywhere near her.

This went on for a little more than three years.

My plan wasn't sophisticated. Really, I read a couple books with pick up lines and techniques and went out to bars 4-5 nights a week — approaching, flirting and failing, pushing and pulling, fucking and floundering for those 36 glorious months of experimentation.

It was self-indulgent. But it was a time of growth and a time of movement.

But a couple of years and a few dozen women later, two things happened. First, I began to realize that rampant drunken sex was fun, but not very fulfilling. And it wasn't exactly affecting the other areas of my life in a healthy manner. I had to back up and evaluate myself, to question why I was sacrificing so much time and effort for superficial pleasures.

The second thing that happened was I grew a reputation locally for my exploits. Soon men whom I had never met were emailing me asking if they could come hang out with me, to see how I interacted with women, to watch me "in action." It was weird at first. But then I decided, sure, why not, just buy my drinks or pay me a bit on the side.

And strangely, I feel like that's where the real journey began. To try and model the internal movement, the opening of those emotional worlds, that burgeoning of a new confidence that had been occurring within myself, and then replicate it in other men.

They say if you want to master something, teach it. And this second journey actually ended up being far more educational than the first. When I went out for myself, it was easy. Half the time I was going out to lose myself, to bury my emotions and hopefully wake up in the arms of a stranger. Sometimes it worked. Sometimes it didn't. And that's really all I knew.

But this second journey had a purpose, had a meaning, and I found myself in need of an intellectual foundation. I couldn't just do it, I had to teach it, explain it, and impart it unto other men and then get *them* to do it.

This led me in a winding, twisted path. It began with entries into and exits out of the so-called "Pick Up Artist" community. I researched social psychology, theories behind attraction, historiographies on human sexuality, went on strip club binges, read books on NLP and cognitive therapy, attended various self-help seminars and taught a few myself, shared hotel rooms with runway models, experimented with touch-healing and had a few alternative therapy mishaps, engaged in gender arguments with feminists, and read every crappy dating book on the market.

As I learned and grew, the coaching grew. What began as a sideshow hobby turned into a business — and a full-time business at that. It soon took me to more than two dozen cities across America, then to countries in Europe, to England and Australia, and I even took field trips as far as Argentina, Brazil, Russia, Israel, and Thailand, where I discovered that much of what I had previously assumed about men and women was merely cultural and not universal.

It was a period of immense education and drive, where I made a clear point to not let my thinking be confined by any previous model or paradigm about masculinity or male/female sexuality.

And after all of that, over ten enriching and challenging years, this is what I've come back with:

There are two movements occurring right now.

The first one is a greater social and emotional movement in western culture. There's a call for a new masculinity that's been lacking for generations now. There's been a void of what men are, what they're supposed to be, how they're supposed to behave, and until now no one has moved to fill that void.

Call it overly ambitious, but this book aims to fill that void, to help create the future models of masculine behavior — models to be attractive, powerful and in control of your relationships with women and with your life in general.

The second movement is happening within you personally. It's an emotional and psychological movement. You're reading this because you want to change. You want to change your interactions and relationships with the women in your life. You want these relationships to improve. You want these relationships to be abundant. You want to feel confident and empowered around women, both those you know and those you don't know but want to meet. You want to feel in control of your

3

relationships with them. You want to be sexual with women without shame or hesitation or regret or pain.

This second movement is an internal movement. It took me a long time to come to grips with that. Although this second movement often begins by changing outer behavior and results in a change of outer behavior — what you say, what you wear, how you move — the process itself is an internal one, a shift in priorities and self-perception, which is then reflected in one's social and romantic life.

Because when you change your beliefs and mindsets, the behavior follows.

This book is designed to guide you through that internal movement. The larger social movement is merely a backdrop and is only briefly explained to give context to your current situation. Your failures with women aren't caused because you say the wrong thing or look like the wrong guy. Words and appearances are merely a symptom of a greater internal problem.

Your failures happen because you grew up emotionally ill equipped to deal with women, and more specifically, intimacy. The words you say and looks you have are merely a side effect of that internal lack of ability.

This isn't just about intellectually understanding how to stand, how to talk, how to behave. This isn't "faking it until you make it." It's deeper than that. This is about intellectually processing the ideas that will cause your emotions to shift, which will then lead to permanent and unconscious changes that transform you into the attractive male you can be.

This is that how-to guide.

This book aims to arm you with the ideas and values that will form that emotional foundation you never received in adolescence, to present the masculine model you and I missed out on.

And once you begin this internal shift, you'll find that the social actions — saying the right thing, knowing when to go for the kiss, knowing how to approach a woman, etc. — they will all begin to fall into place, and fall into place in a more profound and powerful way than simply memorizing some lines or following some sort of arbitrary procedure.

4

The beginning of this book is very theoretical. It's the big picture stuff. I do this because I think it's important to lay a foundation to explain the realities of attraction, gender behavior, and what determines your value on the dating market as a man. As the book goes on though, it becomes more technical and specific, slowly honing in on necessary actions and habits. I believe it's important to explain *why* you should do certain actions and behaviors before asking you to do them.

Part I is an honest look at female attraction based on scientific research and the realistic consequences of that research in modern life.

Part II is an overview of the dating strategy that I recommend to all men who come to me for help. The strategy focuses on polarizing reactions from women to screen for the ones most receptive to your identity as soon as possible. We also address rejection and how to use it to your advantage rather than let it hinder you.

This is a reality-based strategy, not based on fantasies or the frivolities of wanting to sleep with every woman you meet or dating a "perfect 10" by coming up with scripts of pick up lines. These desires are rooted in insecurity and should stay where they belong: in your dreams. Rather, Part II is a long-term strategy built to take a man from "no women in my life" to "lots of amazing women in my life" as quickly as possible, with as little effort as possible.

Part III is the first part of our strategy and covers the first of the Three Fundamentals laid out in Chapter 6, building an enjoyable lifestyle and becoming an attractive man. The steps laid out in this part will be specific but will be long-term goals with long-term benefits.

Part IV covers developing courage and becoming a man of action. Men are expected to initiate in all phases of courtship (the reasons why are explained in Part I) and, therefore, a man who is hesitant, anxious or afraid of initiating will not get very far with most women. The advice laid out in this step will require diligence but provide real and lasting change to those willing to dedicate themselves. These steps are medium-term goals with medium-term benefits.

Finally, Part V will cover the nuts and bolts of communicating more effectively, more attractively, more openly, and more sexually. The steps laid out in this section should have immediate, short-term benefits.

My goal is to provide you with in-depth perspective into your emotions and how you operate while also giving you practical processes for improving yourself and achieving your goals.

If you're looking for a book full of "say this line and then execute touch-plan X4Z-3," then you're going to be disappointed, and not only with this book, you're going to be disappointed with every book that gives advice like that because they are band-aid solutions.

Until you learn to trust your own actions and learn to pursue women with your own unique style and personality, you have learned absolutely nothing.

This book aims to give you your first real education on women and attraction, the education you should have received a long time ago, from a number of sources but never did.

And I'll give you a free preview: it has little to nothing to do with what you're saying. It has everything to do with body, expression, emotion, and movement.

A couple years ago I was in Argentina. There I made one of the most important discoveries in all of my time doing this. I saw a girl at a club sitting by herself. She looked upset. And when I approached her, she didn't get any happier. She didn't speak English and I barely spoke any Spanish at the time. She didn't want to dance and seemed uninterested in talking. She seemed shy and aloof, like something distant invisible was occupying her and despite her best efforts, she didn't know how to unburden herself of it.

Eventually, through some tenacity, I got her to dance, and then to smile. And what I discovered over the next week was how unnecessary words actually are when it comes to seduction.

As she and I danced, we touched and played. I played hand games with her, twirled her, made funny faces and communicated with fake sign language. I held her, caressed her and touched her hair. We drew pictures on napkins for each other. When I put my arm around her and she leaned into me it spoke more than 1,000 conversations. We moved and as that movement drove us closer together physically, we came together emotionally until they were one and the same and we came.

Emerson once wrote, "What you do speaks so loudly I cannot hear what you say." Seduction is the interplay of emotions. Your movement, or lack of movement, reflects and alters emotions, not the words. Words are the side effect. Sex is the side effect. The game is emotions, emotions through movement. If you learn anything from this book, let that be it.

Our culture has become stationary. We spend our time sitting behind desks, behind screens, and in cars. We don't move like we used to and we don't feel like we used to.

Over the course of this book, I'll invite you and hopefully inspire you to move. To get up out of that chair, to go outside, to dare to feel, to experiment and to connect. This will involve getting off your ass, but that's a good thing. And I will help you with that. And if you promise to move, then I promise change. Slowly, your looks will change, your words will change, and your actions will change. And hopefully, maybe something amazing will happen. Your emotions will shift and move and vibrate with them, and the women of the world will feel your resonance and come calling.

Part I: Reality

Chapter 1
Non-Neediness

A man's attractiveness is inversely proportional to how needy he is. The less needy he is, the more attractive he will be to women on average. The needier he is, the less attractive he will be to women on average.

Neediness is when a man places a higher priority on others' perceptions of him than his perception of himself. A needy man's actions and words will therefore be primarily motivated by impressing and winning approval from others. Non-neediness is when a man places a higher priority on his own perception of himself than the perceptions of others. A non-needy man's actions and words will therefore be primarily motivated by embodying his own values and desires.

Neediness, therefore, infiltrates all behaviors because it is what inspires and instigates all behaviors. A lack of neediness also infiltrates all behaviors for the same reason. Because it underlies all of your actions and words, to be non-needy is to be more attractive, in every way. It defines and resonates in everything you say and do, the way you stand, the way you smile, the jokes you tell, the people you associate with, the car you drive, the wine you drink, the jacket you wear.

When people say vague things like, "I like the way he carries himself," or "you just need to believe in yourself," or, "he just has 'it', whatever 'it' is," they are referring to a man's lack of neediness. It exudes from him in everything he does. Paradoxically, a man's lack of need for attention and admiration *is itself* a magnet for attention and admiration. A man's comfort and acceptance of the possibility that some people will not like him makes people like him even more. A man's respect for differing opinions makes those around him want to agree with him more.

A needy man is constantly investing in the perceptions others have in him. He is being extra nice and friendly when he doesn't want to be because he believes he must do this to be liked and loved. He is buying a fancy watch and season tickets to the local sports team so that he will be admired and loved. He is coming up with fake compliments or pretending to be a bad ass because he thinks it will get him attention and love.

A non-needy man may still do these behaviors — he may still buy the season tickets or make the jokes. But his *intentions* are different. Whereas a needy man says and does these things for approval, the non-needy man does them simply for the pleasure of doing. The needy man tries to control what others think and feel more than what he thinks and feels himself. The non-needy man is more concerned with controlling his own thoughts and feelings rather than the thoughts and feelings of others. A needy man will be more invested in the woman he is with than in himself – he will be more concerned about *her* opinion, about him, about the weather, about everything other than what he actually thinks and feels. A non-needy man will be more invested in himself than the woman he's with.

By *investment*, I mean the degree to which you sacrifice/alter your own thoughts, feelings, and motivations for someone else. By *less* I mean that as a man, you should not be willing to sacrifice your thoughts, feelings, and motivations for someone else more than they sacrifice theirs for you.

That may sound cold, un-PC, and yes, it made me squirm a little bit when I first realized it. But it's true.

Think about it, for the majority of human history, men had few material possessions by which women would judge their status. Back in the caveman days, there were no outdoor pools and tax returns. They didn't have brand name sandals and expensive haircuts. At most, one man had a little bit more meat to share than the next guy.

Therefore, for the majority of human history, women watched men's behavior. Ask yourself what kind of behavior would indicate to a woman that a man is high status and fit to raise her children? These are the men who would be sexually selected over the course of hundreds of thousands of years.

Would it be a man who defers to all of the other men around him, who begs the women to be with him, who can't stand up for himself and whose emotions are dictated by those around him? Or would it be the man who controls his own destiny, is unfazed by the threats others may pose to him and who shrugs it off if he pursues a woman and she has no interest in him?

The second man indicates a man of status. If you're at the top of the food chain, you have no reason to be inhibited or to defer to others (unless you want to). If you're at the bottom of the food chain, your entire life will revolve around deferring to others.

The high-status man displays non-neediness. The low-status man displays neediness.

Neediness is not consciously calculated by women or people in general. I guarantee you will not see women walking around with neediness scorecards.

Neediness is a feeling. It's intuited by women. It's instinctual. It's the gag reflex she has when a guy calls her twelve too many times. It's the distaste she has when he seems to laugh a little too hard at her jokes. It's the annoyance she has when he seems to make every decision for her rather than letting her fend for herself.

Women unconsciously detect neediness by sensing the intentions behind a man's behavior and words. It's why women can often become turned off at the most innocuous moment or by the most unimportant statement. Consciously, the action or statement may seem harmless, but unconsciously, it conveyed everything they need to know about your status and that is this: you base your actions on a constant need for approval.

As you are probably aware, women can be needy as well. And although neediness is a turn-off for most men, it's not the complete deal breaker that it is for women.

To most women, a man with no neediness is like a woman with perfect tits and a gorgeously sculpted ass. To a woman, a man with a lot of neediness is like having the worst breath and missing teeth.

It's important to note that non-neediness doesn't mean you should *only* care about yourself. This is narcissism, and although it might get you laid, it is not attractive and will result in dysfunctional relationships.

When you are attracted to a woman, you *should* be affected by her, you *should* be invested in her. That's the whole fun of it! That's the reason we have relationships in the first place, to be touched and moved by others. The important point here is how we prioritize other people's perceptions versus our own. Which is more important? Hers or yours?

Highly needy men will end up in relationships sometimes, but only with highly needy women. The highly needy man is constantly working to earn a woman's approval, and a highly needy woman is constantly in need of a man's approval. So the two conspire together, usually with one creating drama/emotional meltdowns and the other one endlessly fixing it. This relationship is toxic and can harm each person's self-worth.

Narcissistic men, or men who *only* care about themselves, will end up in relationships sometimes, but only with narcissistic and shallow women. Both the narcissistic man and woman will view each other merely as ornaments to adorn their self-absorbed lives. These relationships also are toxic. And these relationships also often end poorly.

Now all this stuff sounds nice. But let's put this into concrete, real-world terms. Here are a couple examples.

James is a nice guy. But he tends to be needy in his relationships and has what we would call a high level of investment with any woman that he meets.

Whenever he dates a woman, he will rearrange his entire schedule at her whim. He will buy her gifts and spend most of his paycheck on the nicest dinners for her. He'll forgo plans with his guy friends and if the woman he dates gets angry, he'll sit patiently and listen to her vent all of her frustrations to him, agreeing with her constantly in a futile desperation that she may feel better. Even when he feels that she's being irrational or treating him unfairly, he won't say anything because he doesn't want her to be upset with him.

As a result, despite caring for him, James's girlfriends rarely respect him. And sooner or later — usually sooner — they dump him. When James gets dumped, he becomes distraught and depressed. He's often inconsolable and drinks too much. Usually, he doesn't feel better again until he meets another woman and the entire cycle repeats itself.

Then there's Jeff. Jeff has been successful with women for his entire life and has a very low level of investment in them until he's gotten to know them well. Jeff enjoys going out with his friends and pays no attention to whether the women around him approve of him or not. At times, he says something weird or gets rejected, but it doesn't bother him.

But other times girls become quite attracted to Jeff. When Jeff notices, if he finds them attractive, he'll take their number and ask them out. When he takes them out, he takes them to the park down the street from his flat. He then sits there and chats with them for a while and if he doesn't like them, he'll excuse himself and leave. If he does like them, he might take them to get ice cream or check out a show with him. If at any point she decides she doesn't like him and leaves, Jeff doesn't really mind. He figures that he wouldn't have been happy with her anyway, so why change himself to please her?

Jeff ends up sleeping with a lot of women. His phone is constantly ringing with texts from them, but he only answers them when he has time or feels like it. He's never rude or nasty to them. But he only makes time for the ones he genuinely enjoys spending time with.

James has a high level of emotional investment in the women he meets and dates. He's not confident. He is needy. He immediately enslaves what little of his identity he's aware of to what he believes will make women like him.

Jeff has a low level of investment. He's content with his life and proud of who he is. He is confident and non-needy. If a woman doesn't appreciate that, then he figures he's better off without her.

Women, as if with a sixth sense, detect Jeff's lower level of emotional investment because it informs all of his decisions and behaviors. Jeff is a high self-esteem individual who takes care of himself and is therefore able to be himself around others. James is not. Within moments of speaking to Jeff, and often even before speaking to him, women sense that not only does he have a strong sense of identity, he's also unwilling to compromise that identity for her. This sub-communicates his high status to them and elicits attraction. How Jeff communicates this will be discussed later in the book.

Ask women and they will tell you that they can immediately tell if a man's "got it," or if he doesn't. They don't know what "it" is, but they know if he has it or not. That "it" that they intuitively know in their gut the second they see him walk, hear him talk, or look him in the eye is his level of investment relative her and, therefore, his lack of neediness.

If this all seems impractical so far, don't worry. The majority of this book is based on how to get "it" and how to convey "it" with women immediately, regardless of what you actually say or do.

The Seduction Process

Biologically, women have a lot more to lose than men when it comes to sex. As a result, they've had incentives to (usually) be pickier in choosing their sexual partners. Men, on the other hand, have historically had fewer repercussions for promiscuity and, from a biological point of view, even gain some advantages by being promiscuous.

Whether it's biological or cultural or some mixture of both, the fact is that female sexual attraction is based largely in feeling comfortable and secure with a man she meets. Women have evolved a sexuality that is more psychological than physical, and that psychological need is rooted in the need for security and connection.

This is why status is based on behavior and not simply assets. A man who is rich in assets has greater potential to make a woman feel secure and comfortable, but if his behavior implies that he won't, then she won't be attracted to him. A physically fit man will imply greater fitness for her children, but again, if his behavior implies he will be incapable or incompetent in raising them, then she will not be attracted to him.

Because men value sex more than women at the beginning of a relationship, and sexual opportunities are scarcer for men than women, women tend to be less invested and more confident early in on the interaction. When a man approaches her and induces her to become *as invested in him as he is in her*, this is the process of seduction. Sex occurs as a natural side effect of this process.

Seduction is the process by which a man induces a woman to become as invested in him as he is in her.

There are two ways for seduction to happen: 1) a man creates the perception that he is far less invested in her than he actually is (neediness disguised as non-neediness), and 2) a man actually is less invested in her (genuine non-neediness).

The first method (a man giving false impressions) occurs through what I call "performance." The vast majority of the dating advice out there for men (and women) is performance-based advice — say this, act like this, don't call her back right away, pretend you don't like her, make these jokes, etc.

16

The second method (a man demonstrating less investment) is a passive process that he does within himself and that permeates every aspect of his behavior over the long-term. There's nothing to learn or memorize. There is nothing to practice or study. It only requires one to move his yardstick for success from external goals (more dates, more sex) to internal goals (better relationships, more emotional fulfillment, overall happiness). This book will lay out how this internal process occurs and how to achieve it in yourself.

Performance-based dating advice technically "works." It's just not fulfilling. You're not actually solving the problem (your neediness); you're just covering it up. A man who becomes successful through a series of performance-based behaviors may have sex, but he is setting himself up for terrible and unfulfilling relationships with other needy women.

Let me take you through a few real-life examples of seduction and look at the various factors going on in each one from a neediness/investment point of view. These examples are real, but identities have been changed and minor details altered.

When Ryan was in college, he was a leading member of his fraternity. He was in charge of organizing his house's parties. He was a gregarious guy and liked by most people. At one of these parties, he met Jane. Jane took an immediate liking to Ryan and the two began dating. Ryan would organize and throw his parties, Jane would come and bring her friends. They shared stories, experiences and interests. The rest of college went on like this.

After they graduated, Ryan took a job at a bank. Jane got involved in a local charity. Ryan's social network disappeared and his long hours at work killed any desire for him to go out and make new friends. He began to spend more and more time with Jane. They usually just watched movies and shared a bottle of wine.

As time went on, Jane became more and more involved in her charity events and began traveling to help with fundraisers. Ryan would spend this time alone watching TV or maybe grabbing a beer with one of his old buddies, but it wasn't the same. After another year, Ryan would openly complain to Jane about her trips. Jane obviously sympathized with Ryan, but she felt pressured and resented him for it. They began to fight more often. Ryan gained weight. Jane spent more time working away from home.

Ryan decided to plan a lavish trip for the two of them to the Caribbean. He could use the much-needed time away from work, and it would infuse their relationship with the excitement and passion that it sorely needed. The trip returned the romance to their relationship briefly. But upon returning home, reality began to set in once again. Within a few months it was back to business as usual: him overworked and irritable, her distancing herself and traveling.

Ryan began talking about marriage. Jane was hesitant. She stated that her job was getting busier and she didn't know how much she'd be around to plan a wedding. Ryan had been saving much of his money to buy her a ring. Jane lamented that they were still young and hadn't really experienced much of life yet. Secretly, in the back of her mind, she couldn't shake the feeling that Ryan was terrified of just that: experiencing life, and marrying her was just another way for him to escape it.

Dejected, a few weeks later Ryan began to complain that Jane spent too much time with her friends and at work. Indeed, Jane had been staying at work until way into the night, even on days when she didn't have to. Ryan began pressuring Jane to move in together, but again she resisted, this time fervently. Ryan exploded, he had been giving up everything for her the past few years and she had been nothing but ungrateful. She retorted that Ryan had been suffocating her with his demands for attention and affection. Jane dumped him on the spot.

There's a good chance the above story sounds familiar to you. You or one of your friends or family members have probably gone through the same process as Ryan: meet girl in a situation of low emotional investment and low neediness, entered relationship with said girl, gradually invested more and more while letting the rest of your personal life slip away, until girl leaves you and dates some other guy who is less invested than she is again.

Here's another story that may sound familiar to you.

Daniel is 24 years old and trying to get over a three-year dry spell. It's the first time he's pursued women since his only girlfriend dumped him three years ago.

Daniel goes out to a bar one night and approaches Stacy. Daniel approaches her with what seems like an innocuous question about drunk guys getting in fights. She responds and he follows it up with a number of quirky lines to soon get her laughing.

These are lines and questions Daniel learned from reading a pick up book on women. Daniel has been practicing the tactics for a while and has recently become proficient at using them. After facing countless rejections, he's finally able to get girls' phone numbers and even a few dates.

He continues to talk to Stacy throughout the night about pre-ordained topics he's comfortable with. He's able to punctuate each lull with tried and tested jokes he's used dozens of times. Every time, Stacy laughs on cue. He touches her on the arm just like he read to do, and she touches him back. She's interested.

A week later, after some fun texting, Stacy meets up with Daniel for a date. Once again, Daniel executes everything he's learned: stick to topics about her passions, move her from venue to venue, never sits across from her but next to her, use a planned excuse to get her back to his place, etc.

There are hiccups along the way, but it all more or less works. Stacy seems genuinely attracted and when Daniel finally works up the nerve to kiss her, she kisses back enthusiastically.

Daniel is ecstatic. He feels like months of hard work have finally paid off.

The second date goes similarly. Daniel manages to get Stacy back to his apartment where, fumbling through his excitement, he has sex with her.

Daniel is on cloud nine, delirious with joy and drunk on validation. He jumps online to talk to his best friend and tell him all of the clever lines he said and how much she likes him.

Little does Daniel realize that it wasn't his lines and tricks that Stacy fell for, it was the endearing way he laughed at himself whenever he was self-conscious. She thought it was cute and it reminded her of her first boyfriend. She also was in a lonely stretch of her life and wanted to feel needed by someone and the fact that Daniel was working so hard for her approval flattered her and made her feel a little less alone.

At least for a little while.

Daniel and Stacy see each other a few more times over the following weeks, but something changes. Since he's already had sex with her, Daniel stops running his lines and tactics that he learned. He slowly reverts back to his normal self, his needy self: desperate for attention and approval.

It begins subtly with him agreeing with everything she says, followed by a sudden inability to come up with new and interesting topics of conversation. It turns out he spends most of his time watching TV and playing video games, and there's not a whole lot to talk about on that front. What used to be vibrant and hilarious bantering has now turned into Stacy showing up, saying whatever she wants and Daniel more or less agreeing with her until it's time to have sex — which is now bad, uninteresting sex.

But Stacy is changing too. She's starting to realize that she used sex as a way to make herself feel less lonely and that perhaps she was way too invested in a guy she actually didn't have anything in common with. But rather than recognize that she made a mistake, she continues to see Daniel out of guilt and for fear of feeling like a slut.

One day, Daniel texts Stacy about meeting up with him that weekend. She was busy studying for a test that night and didn't reply. Stacy *was* actually busy, she tells herself. What she doesn't admit to herself is that she could have made time if she wanted.

Daniel begins to get insecure about why Stacy's not responding. He gets online and asks his friend for advice. His friend says that he needs to text her something really crazy to get her to pay attention and like him again.

The next day, after her test, Stacy sees her phone and notices four new texts from Daniel. The first one is casual, but each one gets progressively weirder and more nonsensical. Stacy is turned off — it's that neediness rearing its ugly head again. But again, out of guilt and unsure of how to end things due to her own neediness, she decides to pretend the texts didn't happen and agrees to meet Daniel that weekend, even though at this point, it feels more like an obligation and not something she's excited to do.

But Daniel is not so easily fooled. He's not about to reward Stacy's "bad behavior" by immediately hanging out with her. He was taught in his pick up books to never let the girl set the terms of the relationship. So he waits a few hours and then texts Stacy that she's too late and he's already made other plans with other people. She finds this strange. Daniel had texted her four times, but truthfully she feels somewhat relieved. She can move on with her life.

The following week Daniel texts Stacy and coldly insinuates that he's ready to see her now, if she's willing to work for it. The condescension and disrespectful tone pisses Stacy off and she doesn't respond.

Two days later Daniel, drunk and confused about why Stacy doesn't want to see him anymore, sends a sappy text saying that he really likes her and really wants to see her again and doesn't know why she doesn't like him anymore.

Completely confused and turned off, Stacy replies that he's a nice guy but she just wants to be friends, even though she has no intention of ever seeing him again.

I can tell you that I've seen both of these stories play out over and over and over again, in hundreds of different forms between hundreds of different people.

Guy meets girl. Guy shows less investment in girl than himself, sex and/or relationship occurs, guy becomes more invested in girl than himself, sex stops and/or relationship falls apart.

The first story is an example of why it's important to continue to invest in oneself even as life changes occur and the relationship goes on. It's the only long-term solution to keep long-term relationships stable and happy.

Ryan's relationship with Jane failed because after he graduated from college, he lost and never regained the great aspects of his identity that made him so attractive to Jane in the first place — his social network, his joy and spontaneity, the cool group activities he planned. As he got cornered into a job he hated and lost his social circle, he began leaning on her more and more to define his identity for himself. He invested less in himself and more and more in her.

Meanwhile, Jane flourished after graduation, quickly falling into a job she was passionate about and good at. She made new friends and began traveling and having new experiences on her own. As Jane became less invested in Ryan for her identity, Ryan became more invested in Jane, growing needier and needier. Eventually, the dynamic of investment shifted and the relationship toppled over.

Daniel's experience was different. Daniel's story is a quintessential example of why pick up lines, routines, value tactics and the like are only short-term solutions. Daniel was needy and highly-invested in Stacy's affection from the start. All Daniel did was use techniques and lines to trick Stacy into thinking he was far more confident and less invested than he actually was.

And it worked, for a bit. But the irony here is that what attracted her the most was not Daniel's lines, but the authenticity of him bumbling through them to impress her. Stacy found it endearing and genuine and was in an unconfident place herself at the time. She was in a place in her life where she wanted to feel needed and powerful. She also found the idiosyncrasies of his personality to be cute, as they reminded her of her first boyfriend. So she slept with him.

But as Daniel's lines and techniques ran out, the true level of investment became more and more clear. Daniel's behavior became erratic and it disgusted Stacy, causing her to cut him off in some ugly text exchanges.

But a lot of men who follow this type of dating advice don't even make it that far. They may conjure the impression of status for only an hour or even a few minutes before they falter. Such are the stresses of performance.

Learning techniques and pick up lines without doing genuine, identity-level work in order to permanently decrease your neediness ends up only being a band-aid solution. It provides a short, temporary relief from an otherwise permanent problem. It causes more stress. And it ultimately makes us feel worse about ourselves.

Overcoming neediness is not about learning what to say or new things to do. Overcoming your neediness comes through a change in your mindset, your self-perception, and your self-respect. It's as simple as just changing your mind about women.

Take a moment to consider…

…That before meeting a woman, instead of worrying whether or not she will like you, you could wonder if you will like her.

…That instead of feeling the need to impress her, you could wonder if she impresses you.

…That instead of sitting there silently wondering what to say next to make her like you, you could sit there silently wondering what she will say to make you like her.

…That instead of waiting around for her to call, you could find something else to do while she waits for your call.

…That instead of worrying if you're tall enough or good-looking enough or skinny enough, you could decide whether they're too superficial to recognize your great qualities.

…That instead of trying to come up with the perfect date, you could decide that a woman who really likes you for you doesn't need a perfect date.

…That instead of looking for a conversation she'll enjoy, you could talk about something you enjoy and see if she takes interest.

…That instead of looking for her approval, you could decide whether or not to give yours.

…That instead of getting upset about why she doesn't want to be with you, you could decide that it means you probably wouldn't want to be with her.

This may all sound a bit selfish. But, in fact, it's called having strong boundaries and high self-esteem. It's called being non-needy and an attractive man.

Only making time for people who make time for you. Only being interested in dating people who are interested in dating you. Worrying about what will make you happy instead of what will make someone else happy. Looking for a person who meets your needs instead of trying to always meet theirs. Changing yourself to become who *you* want to be, not what you think women want you to be.

Because, ironically, that *is* what women want you to be: a man who wants to be who *he* wants to be.

Women are attracted to a man they can respect, to a man they can trust. If you're constantly looking for approval for what to say and how to feel, how could anyone respect or trust you?

You are what attracts (or repels) others — not the words, not the strategies. If you aren't happy with the results *you* get, then it's time to improve *you*.

I don't care how hot she is. Is she good enough for you? Does she have integrity? Standards? Is she smart, personable, caring? Are you ready to leave on a dime if she offends you or breaks your trust?

If not, that's probably why you're not with her in first place.

The only real dating advice is self-improvement. Work on yourself. Conquer your anxieties. Resolve your shame. Take care of yourself and those who are important to you.

Love yourself. Otherwise no, one else will.

Narcissism and Overcompensation

When a man has spent his entire life needy and highly invested, doing the legitimate work to transform himself into a confident, attractive man is not easy.

To become non-needy, a man must develop self-respect, a healthy sense of boundaries, social competence, and healthy life habits. It's often a painful long-term process that entails quite a bit of introspection, questioning, doubt, anger, frustration, lifestyle changes, and so on.

But there is a shortcut. And that shortcut is to objectify women, to treat them as objects or trophies to be accumulated or paraded around for others.

As I said earlier, some men try to fake non-neediness through performance. We've already seen how this ultimately fails in the long run.

But other men overcompensate. It's so hard for them to let go of what others think of them and to stand up for themselves. So they go the complete opposite direction and decide to only care about themselves. They become narcissistic and self-serving, they view their relationships as vehicles to get specific benefits and are unconcerned with the needs of the person they're with.

Needy men only know how to care about what others want, even if it harms themselves. Non-needy men look for that intersection where they can get both their own needs and their partner's needs met. Narcissistic men overcompensate and decide to only pursue getting their own needs met.

Narcissistic men usually do this by conjuring up all sorts of false beliefs about the inferiority or difference of women — how women are incapable of rationality, how they're "hypergamous," how they manipulate men, how women are destined to be dominated and controlled.

It's all bullshit, but these men use it as a justification for their overcompensation to put them at ease in their own self-absorption.

Men who go narcissistic act like they're more important than anybody else. They are aggressive, insensitive, and demanding. They are self-serving and don't handle rejection or loss well. Some of these men even end up becoming abusive.

But the narcissist's façade is weak and transparent. The truth is that the man's narcissism is wielded as a sort of shield to protect the sensitive neediness underneath. See, narcissistic men are still desperate for the approval of others. They've just taken a counterintuitive route to getting it: their own self-aggrandizement. Whereas a needy man will play at being meek and unimportant in order to get approval from others, the narcissist proclaims his own greatness to get approval from others.

When a woman becomes merely another conquest, a number, something to treat like a trophy or a toy, it can be extremely easy to assert yourself around them, to prioritize your own values and beliefs over theirs, to risk rejection around them, and to dominate any perspective they might have — all attractive confident traits, merely expressed in horrible ways.

Narcissism is also taught to men as a form of dating advice. Much of the dating advice out there advises men to be selfish, to be "alpha," to be dominant and aggressive and to ignore women's objections or rejections, to pursue what you want no matter what and take it through pure persistence and aggression. It will justify this advice with all sorts of explanations that women don't actually know what they want, that they're just "testing" you, that they actually want it but they can't say it, and so on.

Narcissism is also often promoted to men by other men growing up, especially in highly "macho" cultures (Latin America, the Middle East, East Asian, etc.). Men are often raised by other narcissistic men who only found their way through relationships through self-aggrandizement and selfishness, and so they seek to pass these traits onto their sons.

Narcissism in a relationship is built on the idea of always being dominant or in control. It is a nebulous mixture of selfishness, assertiveness, and domination that is achieved not through investing more in oneself, but by minimizing the importance of others.

This strategy is ultimately self-sabotaging then. Narcissistic men see seduction and relationships as another competition to be dominated and won, not as a collaboration to be enjoyed. If the goal is to cultivate highly enriching relationships that add to one's life, then minimizing the importance of those around you in order to attract them to you makes the resulting relationships unfulfilling and superficial.

Narcissistic men end up with narcissistic and/or highly needy women. Narcissistic women will use the narcissistic man to aggrandize themselves, to put themselves up and fulfill their own egotistical goals. Needy women will tolerate a narcissistic man's poor treatment of them because the needy woman is constantly in search of a feeling of greatness herself.

And the sad thing is, it works — not on all women, not even on most women, but it will work on women who have no confidence, who expect to be treated like shit, and who treat men like shit in return. Women with any self-worth will pass up on a narcissistic man in a heartbeat. She sees right through his macho veneer. But low self-esteem women, particularly women with truckloads of emotional problems or a history of abuse, will gladly throw themselves onto the narcissistic man and bring him down with them.

So yeah, being narcissistic and overcompensating works. But it leads to unpleasant, shallow, and superficial interactions, constant headaches dealing with women who you don't actually even really like and who probably don't even actually like you, women regretting having sex with you, and emotionally unstable girls who bother you constantly. It's like swimming in the shallow end of the pool — yeah, you're swimming, but it's not nearly as rewarding as the deep end, and there's piss everywhere.

Narcissism comes in many varieties but usually boils down to this: focusing on your own wants and desires to the point of imposing them onto others. Exaggerate your dominance and boast of your strength. Accept no wrongdoing. Admit no faults. Blame others for your problems. Go out of your way to make others feel smaller so that you appear bigger.

The problem with narcissism is that it defines itself by getting what it wants from others. A man who is narcissistic only feels non-needy if he's dominating somebody else and if someone else is giving him what he wants. And in that subtle way, he is therefore more invested in others than he is in himself. He is therefore still needy and unattractive.

To give an example, if a non-needy man meets a woman who rejects him or is not interested in him, he will assume that is was either an incompatibility or that it was just not the right situation. Either way, he will see it as the right thing to have happened. His life will go on.

But when a narcissistic man is rejected, he becomes angry and hurt. He blames the woman for not seeing his greatness. He calls her stupid or selfish or shallow because she's not willing to give him what he – a random guy talking to her – wants.

It's just another form of performance — he acts as if he's in control, but his desperation to be in control is due to insecurity. A non-needy man doesn't try to control what women feel about him. Rather he tries to control what he feels about certain women. He understands that the world isn't about him and that all he can control is himself and his own actions. He's not bothered when things don't go his way or when people don't recognize him as being amazing because he already feels amazing himself. He doesn't need their approval and their disapproval doesn't faze him from his mission.

Narcissistic men are often serial players, guys who obsessively seek out casual sex and not only regard the women they sleep with poorly, but treat them poorly as well.

Let's do another example:

Roy was a nice guy all through college. He was a geeky science guy but adored by all of the girls he hung out with. Roy adored them as well, but in a sexual way. Unfortunately, whenever Roy worked up the nerve to say something, they always told him they just wanted to be his friend. All the while, Roy would sit there listening to his female friends complain about their horrible and insensitive boyfriends. All Roy could think was, "But I care about you, I'm sensitive, and I'm right in front of you. Why can't you see that?"

Needless to say, Roy's female friends never came around. Despite all of the waiting and hoping and placating, they always moved on to the next guy — usually a guy they had just met.

27

Eventually, when Roy was 25 years old, he landed his first girlfriend: a depressive and slightly overweight grad student who worked in his lab. Despite her obvious shortcomings, he was smitten with her. But his girlfriend's emotional instability eventually got the best of both of them. After a turbulent year together, they broke up.

Roy's anger boiled over. He was sick of being walked over and kicked around. He was sick of being ignored and hurt. His entire life, women had never paid attention to him sexually, and the one who finally did wasn't satisfied. Roy decided he had had enough, that it was time to put himself first. It was time to put his own needs first. He saw how other men had been assholes to his female friends and slept with them, so he decided that he would do the same.

Roy quickly found that he was comfortable dishing out insults and teases toward the women he talked to. It felt like vindication for a lifetime of emotional negligence. Some women were offended, but strangely this made Roy feel even more powerful and motivated him to go out and meet even more women.

Soon, to Roy's surprise, some of these girls actually became attracted to him. He took them home and slept with them. At first, the girls were drunk and ugly, but slowly and surely, as Roy became more comfortable in his new player persona, the girls became more attractive.

Some of the girls Roy slept with were genuinely intrigued by Roy and wanted to get to know him better. Roy would toy with these women, play phone tag with them, use them for sex a few more times and then invent some sort of conflict or blame her for something she didn't do as an excuse to not see her anymore. These women quickly got the picture that Roy was neither stable nor an enjoyable person to spend time with, so they moved on.

Other girls Roy slept with weren't as intrigued with him as they were emotionally desperate for some sort of male validation.

Some of these women simply wanted to be validated by having sex. In which case, Roy fucked them and never heard from them again.

But for many others, their neediness was deeper than that. These women desperately craved emotional validation as well as sexual validation. They would launch into crying fits, call Roy dozens of times over the course of a night or show up at his apartment unannounced. The sex was often

28

incredible, but it was almost impossible for Roy's own anger and insecurities to not get sucked into the drama of these other women. Dramatic episodes would go on for weeks or sometimes months in a cycle of angry breakup, back to loving reunion, back to angry breakup, over and over again, each time getting more intense. Many of these women had experienced sexual abuse in their past. Eventually, Roy would tire of their games and break things off permanently, swearing to never let himself succumb to them again. But often the next "crazy" girl would be right around the corner.

I always tell men, if every girl you date is unstable and crazy, that's a reflection of *your* emotional maturity level. It's a reflection of *your* confidence or lack of confidence. It's a reflection of *your* neediness. Non-needy people don't date needy people and vice-versa. They can't because there's no attraction to begin with.

If all of the women you attract are needy and emotionally helpless, what does that say about you?

Roy went from being needy to overcompensating with narcissism. He went from worshipping women with no respect for himself to worshipping himself with no respect for women. The key to non-neediness is to have both: respect for both oneself *and* for women.

The only permanent way to attract and date more women and more attractive women is to become more attractive yourself. And the way a man becomes more attractive himself is by investing in himself, in becoming less needy.

Permanent change to one's investment and neediness in one's relationships with women is hard and is a process that encompasses all facets of one's life. But it's a worthwhile journey. As a man, it may be *the most* worthwhile journey.

And the key to it is probably something you wouldn't expect. In fact, it's something that most men turn their nose up at when they hear it. The key is vulnerability.

Chapter 2
Power in Vulnerability

When most men hear the word "vulnerability," their immediate reaction is to associate it with weakness. In general, men are raised to withhold their emotions, to not show weakness, and to ignore any hint of introspection. On top of that, most of the popular dating advice out there encourages guys to be aloof, standoffish, judgmental, and at times, scathing towards women.

Men have a lot of negative assumptions about the idea of being more vulnerable and opening up to their emotions. Chances are it makes you a little skeptical or queasy to even see me writing about this.

Don't worry, I'm not going to have you hold hands around a campfire with some wimpy support group and cry about your spirit crystal or share stories about your power animal.

I want you to think of vulnerability in a more broad way. Not just emotional vulnerability (although we'll get to that), but physical vulnerability, social vulnerability.

For instance, making yourself vulnerable doesn't just mean being willing to share your fears or insecurities. It can mean putting yourself in a position where you can be rejected, saying a joke that may not be funny, asserting an opinion that may offend others, introducing yourself to a group of people you don't know, telling a woman that you like her and want to date her. All of these things require you to stick your neck out on the line emotionally in some way. You're making yourself vulnerable when you do them.

In this way, vulnerability represents a form of power, a deep and subtle form of power. It's courageous, even. A man who's able to make himself vulnerable is saying to the world, "Screw the repercussions; this is who I am, and I refuse to be anyone else." He's saying he is non-needy and high status.

Most people think of a man who's vulnerable as a man who cowers in the corner and begs others to accept him or not hurt him. This is not vulnerability; this is surrender. It's weakness.

Think of it this way, there are two men. One stands tall, looks straight ahead. Looks people in the eye when he speaks to them. Says what he thinks and is comfortable if some people disagree with him. When he makes a mistake, he shrugs it off and apologizes if necessary. When he sucks at something, he admits it. He's unafraid to express his emotions, even if that means he gets rejected because of them sometimes. He has no problem moving on to people who don't reject him, but instead like him for who he is.

The second man hunches over, his eyes dart around and he is unable to look someone in the eye without getting uncomfortable. He puts on a cool persona that is always aloof. He performs. He avoids saying things that may upset others, and sometimes even lies to avoid conflict. He's always trying to impress people. When he makes a mistake, he tries to blame others or pretend like it didn't happen. He hides his emotions and will smile and tell everyone he's fine even when he's not. He's scared to death of rejection. And when he is rejected, it sends him reeling, angry, and desperate to find a way to win back the affection of the person who doesn't like him.

Which one of these two men is more powerful? Which one is more vulnerable? Which one is more comfortable with himself? Which one do you think women would be more attracted to?

From an evolutionary perspective, vulnerability makes perfect sense as an indicator to women of male status and fitness. Let's say there's a tribe of 20 men, all hunter-gatherers, all men with more or less equal possessions (or lack thereof).

Some of the men in the tribe are constantly reactive to what the other men tell them. They don't admit faults. They change their behavior and what they say to win the approval of the other men. When something doesn't go their way, they look to blame someone else. What would this say about their status in their tribe? If they're basing all of their behavior on the approval of the other men and are constantly covering up their weaknesses, it says that they're low status, not trustworthy, unconfident, and probably not going to be a dependable father.

Now imagine other men in the same tribe who are unfazed by the neediness or temper tantrums of the other men around them. They focus purely on the task at hand and don't change their behavior based on what others think of them. When challenged, they stand up for themselves, but when they're wrong, they also admit their fault since they see no reason to hide their weakness. They have a sense of honor. They don't react to any of the other men around them; rather, the other men react to them.

This behavior implies high status, a man who is dependable, comfortable in his strengths and weaknesses, a man who can be counted on and who is likely to rise through the ranks and provide for his offspring.

He's likely to succeed and likely to be a dependable father.

It's likely that women have been naturally selected to choose high-status men based on their *non-neediness* first, and then their looks and accomplishments second, since looks and accomplishments tend to be reflections of non-needy behavior, not the other way around. This non-needy behavior indicates a man who is comfortable with vulnerability, who isn't afraid to express who he is, warts and all, to the world. This plays out in multiple arenas — in the life decisions he makes (Part III), the extent of his courage (Part IV) and the way he communicates to others (Part V).

Chances are, if you're reading this and are bad with women, then you're bad with women because you don't express your true feelings and intentions very well. Perhaps you're afraid to introduce yourself to women you find attractive or to ask them out on a date. Perhaps you consistently fall into boring conversation topics because they're "safe" and shallow and you don't have to risk offending or inciting anyone with them. Perhaps you don't assert yourself and your desires enough. Perhaps you hide from your own sexuality and become scared or nervous when people expose theirs. Perhaps you're stuck in a job or lifestyle you don't truly enjoy because other people always told you that it was a good idea and you didn't want to upset or disappoint the people around you. Dressing extremely well makes you feel uncomfortable, smiling at strangers makes you feel creepy, and the idea of hitting on a woman openly scares you because of the possibility of rejection.

All of these are symptoms of a root problem: an inability to be vulnerable.

Many men, like you, and like me, were raised in such a way as to not express our emotions freely. For whatever reason — maybe our home situation, maybe childhood trauma, maybe our parents didn't express their emotions either — we've grown up with deeply embedded habits designed to keep us stifled and bottled up. Don't be controversial. Don't be unique. Don't do anything "crazy" or "stupid" or "selfish."

I was the same way. For my entire young life, I was terrified of anyone not liking me. The mere thought of someone hating me, girl or guy, would literally keep me up at night. As a result, every aspect of my life revolved around people-pleasing, hiding my faults, covering my tracks, and blaming others. And needless to say, I barely had any success with women. And when I did finally get a girlfriend, she left my ass for a man who could actually express himself.

This all may sound hokey and new-agey. Trust me, it's not. Connecting with women in this way, by being vulnerable — as opposed to performance or narcissism — will result in some of the best interactions and relationships of your life.

Vulnerability is the path of true human connection and becoming a truly attractive person. As psychologist Robert Glover once said, "Humans are attracted to each other's rough edges."

Show your rough edges. Stop trying to be perfect. Expose yourself and share yourself without inhibition. Take the rejections and lumps and move on because you're a bigger and stronger man. And when you find a woman who loves who you are (and you will), revel in her affection.

But opening yourself up to vulnerability, training yourself to become comfortable with your emotions, with your faults, and with expressing yourself without inhibitions doesn't happen overnight. This entire book can be viewed as a how-to guide for vulnerability. But it's a process, and at times, a grueling one.

The Pain Period

When undertaking any emotional shift or change in behavior, there's going to be an initial "pain period." The pain period typically happens in the beginning of the change and forming a new habit. It's the period of greatest resistance and discomfort and the period in which most people give up.

Whether it's bodybuilding, learning a new language or starting a new job, there's going to be an awkward and difficult period where you're going to struggle, fail at times, and most of all, feel vulnerable.

Most people absolutely hate this feeling and avoid it as much as possible. Being vulnerable hurts. It's embarrassing. It's difficult. And as a result, these people don't learn new things or improve the old ones. That first time you approach a woman at a party or offer your number, chances are you're going to be freaking out. And if she doesn't react well, it's going to be quite painful. And that's all right. That first time you pick up the phone to call a girl you like. The first time you go in for the kiss. These are nerve-wracking moments that are not very pleasant to go through.

It's especially difficult if you've already had success in the past through performance or narcissism. Practicing vulnerability often means that you will have to "get worse before you get better."

And chances are, the more you've bottled up your emotions throughout your life, the more painful these actions are going to be. As vulnerability researcher Brene Brown says, "The less you talk about your shame, the more of it you have."

This book presents myriad ways in which to become more vulnerable: how to express yourself better through dress, through conversation, through humor, through your sexuality.

And I can tell you right now, you're going to feel uncomfortable. You're going to come up with rationalizations about how you don't really have to do *that*, do you? How I don't know what I'm talking about. How you're too busy or you will get to it later. You'll plan ahead, procrastinate and then re-plan and then procrastinate again, and then decide you need to read this book a couple more times — all because you're scared to death of simply being vulnerable.

Maybe you've already been through this. Maybe you've already spent months or years avoiding taking action because you're afraid of the consequences. Maybe you've put off that career change, that wardrobe upgrade, joining that dating site. Maybe you've missed opportunities with women who liked you because you were too afraid to make a move. Maybe you convinced yourself that you needed to "know how" first. Maybe you convinced yourself that you needed to see someone else do it first.

These are all forms of avoidance. And they all come from a deep-seated neediness, and that neediness can only be cured through making yourself more vulnerable. And at first, that vulnerability is going to hurt.

You can't skip it. The only way out of it is through it.

I'll give you two examples from my own pain period when I was first learning to open myself up and become vulnerable. Two girls, let's call them Melina and Kate. Melina may have been the first girl I dated after my disastrous break up in 2005. She and I had great natural chemistry and would sit around and talk for hours. But little did I realize how angry I was and how much baggage I was carrying around from my ex.

So one night, talking with Melina, I just went off — for like 15 minutes straight, about my stupid whore of an ex, and went into minute detail about all the fucked up stuff she did, just on and on and on and on. So bitter and hurt. So unnecessary.

I finished. I hadn't even realized how long I had gone on rambling. Then after an awkward silence, Melina looked at me as if scared by something and calmly said, "I probably didn't need to know all of that."

Ouch.

She and I quickly fell apart and stopped seeing each other. I was mortified. I ran into her a number of times after that for months and I would always feel nauseous with embarrassment.

But as awful as this experience was, it was important. It was the first time I had opened up about my feelings about my relationship. And I noticed that in the future I became much more comfortable talking about it. And once I was comfortable talking about it, I began to notice things I had done wrong in that relationship, ways that I could be a better man and a better partner. But for me to get there, I had to be willing to take that first awkward, vulnerable step.

Then there was Kate. Kate was slightly older than me and extremely sexual. Our "first date" was her calling me on the phone and flat out saying, "I want you to come to my apartment and fuck me on my kitchen counter."

"Uhh... OK, sounds good." I played it cool. I was terrified in my head, though. Girls really do this stuff? What does this mean? She barely even knows me.

So I get over there. I'm freaking out, all up in my head, and I can't even keep it up long enough to get it in her. Once again, completely mortified. This had happened with other girls before, but I had always been drunk so I had an excuse. It was the alcohol, not my own twisted, fucked up head.

But no excuse this time. As Kate sat there naked on her kitchen counter, both expectant and horribly disappointed, I became cornered. I had to own up to my own fears. I wasn't such a badass playboy, nor some smooth motherfucker. No, I was a nervous dude with a lot of sexual insecurities and emotional baggage. So I owned up to it. I told her that I was inexperienced and was just coming out of a major dry spell and that I was really nervous. I could see her attraction for me spiral away.

Fortunately, Kate was much cooler with my insecurities than Melina was. She said she understood, to relax, take my time, let her know or whatever. And then I did the super, lame beta thing that every pick up book told me to never, ever, ever do: I asked her if we could get to know each other better first.

Again, it went against everything a "real man" was supposed to do. But it was vulnerable and it was true.

And we did. And then we had sex later, once I had calmed down and was comfortable. She was supportive and didn't hold it against me. And we went on to date for months and have wild and crazy sex on all sorts of furniture around the house. It was amazing. I just needed that time to open up and relax. I dated her on and off for almost a year. The sex was great. And she was a great friend.

Obviously, your issues and neediness are going to be different. My point in all of this, though, is that early on, when the neediness and vulnerability come out, it's awful. It's not sexy. In fact, it's usually incredibly unattractive and uncomfortable.

But that's part of the process. The Pain Period. Slowly, you become comfortable with it. You become unattached to it. And then you become OK with it. The things I just wrote above embarrassed me to the point that I wanted to die when they happened. Now I can talk about them

37

without shame or regret. And these are the types of stories that I'll often share with new women when I date them, told in a similar fashion.

"I was embarrassed. Yes, it sucked. Yes, I have issues. No, I'm not perfect." The implication being the whole time that I'm fine with it. I'm not looking for sympathy or validation. I don't need anything from her. It's just who I am, rough edges and all.

We all have weaknesses, embarrassments, and vulnerabilities. A needy man is terrified to show them because he cares more about what others feel about him than what he feels about himself. A non-needy man is comfortable showing his flaws because he's more comfortable with how he feels about himself than how others feel about him.

Sharing yourself openly with others forces that transition between the two: from needy and afraid of what others think, to non-needy and comfortable in how you feel about yourself. The reason is because sharing these truths about yourself forces you to own them and accept them, and also demonstrates that feeling embarrassed or ashamed is just that, just another feeling, another part of your humanity, not the end of the world.

The real question is, do you have to work through this emotional baggage and neediness with the women you're dating? Not necessarily. You can work through them by sharing them with friends, family members, or a therapist. But there are some issues that can only be dealt with by women you're seeing: particularly intimacy and sexual issues.

But slowly, you will chisel away at yourself. You'll humble yourself, expose yourself, and then learn that it's OK. It's OK to be rejected. It's OK to make mistakes. It's OK to say something stupid. Don't give up. Women will not dislike you for your rejections and mistakes or saying something stupid.

They'll like you for your ability to be OK with being rejected, to make mistakes, and to say something stupid. The man who always has the perfect line to say to her is a man she will not trust because he shows no vulnerability and his words are inauthentic and, therefore, needy.

The man who has some good lines and some bad lines and is able to admit the latter and laugh at the former, this is a man she will trust and a man she will open herself up to, both emotionally and physically. Become comfortable with being imperfect. It's your rough edges she'll be attracted to.

This isn't pretty at first. The worst part of the pain period is the fact that most people who have been stifling their emotions their entire lives have a lot of pent-up anger, frustration, and shame. Typically, the older you are, the more you have pent up. And when you start to express this anger and shame, the uglier it gets.

You may find yourself behaving irrationally, developing strange beliefs, or becoming angry with many people. In many cases, this is why I encourage men who struggle deeply with vulnerability to see a therapist who can perhaps guide them through this process.

You may be reading this and thinking, "Well, that's all fine, but I already express myself really well and am pretty aware of my emotions."

Really?

See, I don't buy it. In all of my years doing this, the single common thread between every man I've worked with who has problems with women is either a lack of awareness of his own emotional motivators or an inability to express his emotions freely with those around him. And the sad part is, almost all of these men think they're fine. We always think that we're the ones who are fine. It's everyone else who is screwed up.

But I'll say this: if you consistently find it difficult to keep a woman interested in conversation; if you suffer from large amounts of anxiety around women; if you constantly feel a need to prove something to others or yourself, then there's something there. Trust me, there's something there. And there's something you're not expressing or some emotion you're not in touch with. And that's fine. We all go through it.

Ultimately, what women want — what we all really want — is a strong, independent, non-needy partner who fulfills us, who we can share ourselves with and receive them in return.

Because sharing yourself with someone doesn't mean just physically occupying the same area. It doesn't mean exchanging facts with one another. It means opening up about your values, desires, feelings, and dreams. It means exposing your shame and insecurities and doubts and fears. It means living with somebody on an emotional plane, inhabiting that same heart-space together because that's the one thing we can't ever achieve by ourselves.

But there's a catch. Many men, when they finish this chapter or hear this whole vulnerability spiel, their first reaction is to say, "Oh, OK, so I'll tell her all of these sob stories and she'll want to have sex. Got it."

No. Wrong. It's not about words or behaviors, it's about *intentions*. So if you're going around telling sob stories and talking about insecurities to get laid, women will sense that and you will be a creep. That is not vulnerability; that is merely another form of performance. And all performance is neediness.

Similarly, if you go around saying and doing whatever you want around women in the name of "expressing yourself," this, too, will not "work" because your intention is not to connect with her and get to know her, but rather simple self-gratification. This is not vulnerability, this is narcissism. And all narcissism comes from neediness.

Stop looking at communication as the surface information and instead, pay attention to the emotions and motivations behind everything that you do and say. That's where all of the meaning is.

I'll say this again because this often gets lost: vulnerability is not a technique or tactic. It is a way of being. It's not something you learn, it's a mindset you practice.

Sometimes I get emails from men saying something like, "Hey, I told this girl all about my dog dying and how I hate my mom. She didn't have sex with me. Vulnerability doesn't work."

And when I get these emails, I shake my head. He doesn't get it. "Doesn't work," he says.

Here's a piece of advice: if you ever find yourself thinking, "That didn't work," or "This doesn't work," then you are performing and you are needy. Point blank. Period.

The whole idea of something "working" on women, is itself a form of neediness. Because a sexual connection is not something you achieve. It's not a level in a video game that you beat. It's not something you can strategize. It's either there or it's not.

When women emotionally connect with you and your desire for them, it's not what you're saying or the words you're choosing, it's the emotion behind those words. If the emotion behind your words is needy and self-

40

serving, then she will become turned off no matter what you say, even if you're telling her the most personal or heartfelt story. If the emotion behind your words is genuine and vulnerable, then it will turn her on, even if you're talking about your grocery list or how you named your dog. Yes, you can fake this stuff in the short-term if you become a good actor. But obviously, don't do that. We're not in this for short-term fixes, remember?

So the catch is that your statements must be authentic. Your statements towards women must be unconditional, otherwise it's not really being vulnerable. If you tell a woman that she's beautiful only because you think it'll give you a better chance of sleeping with her, then amazingly, she will not be very flattered. Try it. It's true. Give women false compliments and see how they respond. They won't respond very well.

But communicate with honest appreciation and you'll be amazed how she lights up in front of you.

So the catch is that everything you say must be as authentic as possible. There's no shortcut. There are no tricks. You say it because you mean it and mean it because you say it. The more nervous it makes you, the better, because it means you're being authentic and making yourself vulnerable.

How attractive you are is based on your lack of neediness. Your non-neediness is based on how vulnerable you're able to make yourself. And how vulnerable you're able to make yourself is based on how honest you are to yourself and others.

Which brings us to our next chapter: the gift of truth.

Chapter 3
The Gift of Truth

"Hey honey, can I pee in your butt?"

I stood there horrified as my friend shouted this at literally every attractive girl who came within five feet of us.

The year was 2006. I was in college, and at the time, to help myself get better with girls, I started hanging out with a couple guys who got more women than anyone else I knew. I was young and naïve and needy and still saw relationships in terms of performance. The idea, then, was that I'd go out with these super player guys, study what they said to women and then emulate it to be successful myself.

Enter my friend Matt and "Can I pee in your butt?"

Matt was a guy I briefly met once through a friend, but his reputation was widely known. He was in a rock band, had tattoos down his arms, and banged girls like it was his part-time job. I had run into him by chance a week or two earlier and this was my first time hanging out with him for a whole night.

As you can imagine, his "Can I pee in your butt?" comment wasn't entirely successful. In fact, I think just about every girl ran away from us in horror. Matt was drunk and I was seriously questioning what the hell I was doing out with him.

But then something funny happened. A couple girls laughed. And then suddenly another girl actually hung around and kept talking to us.

Needless to say, back in 2006, there hadn't been anything written in pick up manuals that I had studied about how to transition out of a "Can I pee in your butt?" opener. So I stood there awkward and confused, waiting to see how this would turn out.

Next thing I know Matt is telling her he's going to lick her butthole tonight…

OK, forget this, I'm going home. I don't want to be associated with this clown when he gets us thrown out of the bar, or worse, arrested for sexual harassment.

About fifteen minutes later, Matt finds me, and surprisingly he's got his arm around the girl he had been talking to. She's got a huge smile across her face.

"Hey man, we're heading back to her place, it was great hanging out, we should do it again sometime."

I sat there in the bar alone, trying to piece together what I had just seen. It made no sense and went against everything I had ever known about women my entire life.

To this day, this was one of the most pivotal nights for me as far as understanding attraction is concerned. Was it that I learned that "Can I pee in your butt?" is the right thing to say?

No, actually, I still think it's a pretty awful thing to say. And truth be told, in hindsight my friend Matt had a lot of narcissism going on.

But what I learned is that regardless of what you say to a woman, the intention and implications of *why* you are saying it are far more powerful than the words themselves.

You can say the lamest and grossest (or funniest, depending on your perspective) thing to women, and if the sub-communication is, "I really don't care if you laugh or run away horrified, but here's who I am, take it or leave it," this sub-communicates a rock-bottom level of investment and an incredibly high level of vulnerability.

Does this mean that saying grotesque things to women for no other reason than to self-amuse will get you laid? Not always. And not necessarily often. But you could do worse.

Does it mean that you should go out and try and say things like this? To "fake it 'til you make it" with this line and other offensive lines? Well, actually, no. Do you know why?

Most men can relate to the idea of trying to "pick up" a woman without looking like they're trying. Or trying to be cool without looking like they're trying to be cool. Entire books and schools of dating advice have been built on this idea — pursuing a woman without actually letting her know that you're interested in her.

Just typing that paragraph feels exhausting. Talk about a lot of work for nothing.

Like I described before, this performance-based stuff works sometimes, but it's a short-term solution that requires a lot of time and effort. In my opinion, it's a terrible investment of time and effort. You may as well invest that time and effort in yourself and let your identity and honesty do all of the attracting for you.

After all, why learn how to fake being cool, when you can just learn to become cool yourself?

On top of that, walking the tightrope of pursuing her without looking like you're pursuing her requires a lot of attention and effort. You can slip up easily. It's very unforgiving and ultimately, not a very enjoyable process. Besides, all of the attention and effort on "gaming" women this way ironically encourages you to be even more highly-invested and needy, therefore decreasing her likely attraction for you.

Men avoid demonstrating an honest interest in a woman because they believe it will signify that they are too invested in her — i.e., it will show that they are needy. They think that when you say, "You're cute and I wanted to meet you," that translates roughly to, "Hi, I'm such a desperate loser that I'm just going to throw all of my desires out there right now and beg you to accept them."

But remember, it's not the actual behaviors or words themselves, it's the *intentions* behind those words. There's a world of sub-communication going on behind a man's honest declaration of his interest. And it's an attractive one.

Because when a man comes right out and says he's interested in a woman, the sub-communication is actually, "I'm totally OK with the idea of you rejecting me, otherwise I would not be approaching you in this manner. Therefore, I'm comfortable with myself and my prospects."

Think about it, if a guy wasn't comfortable with the prospect of a woman rejecting him, he wouldn't have been honest in the first place. In fact, he would have pretended that he wasn't actually interested in her!

The fact that he honestly expressed to her his intentions, that he put his nuts on the chopping block and made himself vulnerable to her immediately, actually sub-communicates non-neediness and attractiveness in itself. And on top of that, it shows desire for her, which is going to trigger her arousal.

Remember: what you actually say doesn't matter; *why* you say it matters.

Always. No exceptions. You can have the best line in the world, but if you're saying it because you're needy and desperate for validation and approval from women, then she is immediately going to sense it.

This is why using pick up lines is ultimately a futile process. I could sell you the best 100 things I've ever said to women, but I can't ever sell you my intentions or my confidence in myself. You must develop those on your own. And once you do, the actual lines you say will be personal and congruent *to you* and nobody else.

The Truth Is Always Shining Through

I'll go ahead and tell you that I actually did go out and say "Can I pee in your butt?" to women the next week. Can you guess what happened?

Nothing.

In fact, I got a bunch of weird and disgusted looks and not a single laugh.

It's because I was saying it looking for a reaction. Once again, I was highly invested in how women responded to me. I simply did not get it at the time. It didn't matter what I said or didn't say; if I said it in a way that demonstrated I cared way too much about how they responded to me, it would never work. I would come off as a creep and women would avoid me as if I had gonorrhea on my face.

This is because the truth is always shining through. You can't fake vulnerability and you can't fake honesty. By their very definition, it's impossible.

Men's dating advice gives women very little credit when it comes to this. Women are generally quite intuitive to emotions, motivations, and social cues. We may think we're clever when we come up with a cute line to approach a woman with, thinking that she has absolutely no idea that we're secretly hitting on her. She does. They always do. And it's not a big deal either.

And not only does she know we're hitting on her, the fact that we seemed so concerned about getting rejected turns her off. The fact that we had to contrive lines and fake stories in order to start a conversation with her, whether consciously or not, signals to her that we are highly invested and not a truly attractive man.

You cannot fake non-neediness for more than a moment. The only women you will manage to fake are women who are drunk or who are extremely needy themselves. Truth.

Non-needy and truly high-quality women who are not invested in the attention they receive from men are not going to have much patience for your lines and games. They will either see through them and see you for who you really are — scared to expose your vulnerability — or they will simply assume you're not worth investing in because you'd rather just talk about spells or games or whatever.

Vulnerability requires honesty, and honesty only works if it's given unconditionally, with no strings attached. That means everything you say and do must be done without any ulterior motive. You are simply expressing your thoughts and feelings as they come to you, without inhibition, without shame.

The truth is always shining through. Even if you lie about yourself or act a certain way, this is actually saying much more about you and your character than the content of your statements. Even if you are exaggerating or putting on a bit of an act to impress a person, your intentions will always shine through, eventually, and they will say more about you than any word ever could.

You can tell women that you're a record producer and are friends with Jay-Z, but chances are unless you're a really good actor, people are going to sense subtle inconsistencies in your behavior to back that up. Sooner or later, they will. Then your true identity will shine through, your lack of vulnerability with shine through, your desperation for affection will shine through, and you will be a sad, pathetic and unattractive man.

This is an extreme example, but it plays itself out the same way on a smaller scale. Let's take a classic example of pretending not to be interested in a woman to get her interested in you.

47

If you pretend you don't like a woman, ignore her, act like what she says is stupid or uninteresting, when in fact you do like her, and you are interested in what she says, subtle cues in your behavior and body language will slowly but surely tip you off. The armor will crack. It may be laughing too much at your own joke. Or tilting your head away at an awkward moment. Or making an awkward comment to her friend that feels forced. But people's bullshit detectors will eventually go off, and you'll be exposed for not presenting an honest expression of yourself.

But what about men who gush about how beautiful a woman is to flatter her? What about the men who buy women drinks and beg them for dates and call them incessantly and tell them how they're always thinking about them? Those guys are being honest about their intentions and their feelings, but they're not getting anywhere, are they?

Here's the problem: human nature is such that we don't trust people who like us if we don't feel as though we earned it somehow. Imagine if some stranger came up to you, started complimenting you incessantly, buying you things, how would you react?

You'd probably think to yourself, "OK, what's this guy selling?" Or maybe, if he was particularly pushy and weird, "Jesus, is this guy an ax murderer?"

That's because they're showing how invested they are in your approval without them actually knowing you, without them taking the time to connect with you and understand you. And as a result, you don't trust them. You find them creepy and weird.

Welcome to every day of an attractive woman's life.

Men like this are broadcasting their neediness like a giant neon billboard coming out of their ass. They come up and gush to a woman about how amazing she is while they've only known her for 10 seconds. They buy her things with only knowing her for a few hours. What this man is signaling to her is, "I don't know you, but I'm already going to do anything to win your approval, that's how desperate I am." And it comes across as pathetic.

And even on a deeper level, what these men are sub-communicating is something else: "The only value I have to offer as a man is money and compliments. I have nothing else going for me."

A man with an attractive and interesting lifestyle, a man with high standards for himself and the relationships in his life, will take the time to get to know an attractive woman before soliciting her with gifts. He will wait until he feels strongly enough to genuinely give her a compliment. And if he talks to her and discovers that there is little that is interesting about her beyond her looks, then he will lose interest.

Ironically, it's these high standards and self-regard that women pick up on and find incredibly sexy. And it's these same standards and self-regard that most men spend a lot of time trying to fake.

When in doubt, check your intentions.

Think about it: the average guy at the bar who goes around buying cute girls drinks — why is he buying them? So the girls will sit there and talk to him. When he comments on how beautiful they are and how he's so infatuated with them, why is he complimenting them? So that they'll like him. When he pays for fancy dinners and offers to buy them jewelry, why is he doing it? So they'll be impressed with him and not leave him.

These are not gifts or compliments at all. These are deals he's brokering. The terms may be implied or unspoken, but they're transactions all the same. Everything he gives to her, he is giving with the expectation to receive something in return. The drinks are not unconditional. They're bought with the provision that she stays and talks to him. The compliments are spoken with the provision that she shows him affection in return.

And when the women don't show appreciation or don't reciprocate interest, he becomes furious, blaming the women for being gold-digging, lying whores and bitches. Again, being a "nice guy" is never much different than being a narcissist. One only gives. The other only takes. But both are the same in their desperation for approval.

This is a subtle form of manipulation and, therefore, at its core, dishonest.

Once again, most high value, confident women will see through this immediately and not hang around a man who does this. In fact, the only women who will go for a man like this are women who are superficial and willing to trade their affection for material and superficial gain — these women are soulless and suppress their emotions as much, if not more than the men who buy things for them.

49

An attractive man expresses his interest unconditionally, expecting nothing in return. This arouses women and when they do reciprocate his interest, their interest is, in fact, a gift in return.

True honesty is only possible when it is unconditional. The truth is only the truth when it is given as a gift — when nothing is expected in return. When I tell a girl that she is beautiful, I say it not expecting anything in return. Whether she rejects me or falls in love with me isn't important in that moment. What's important is that I'm expressing my feelings to her *in that moment*.

I don't use my compliments as a bargaining tool. I give them unconditionally. A needy man will give a woman a compliment without knowing her and wait expectantly for her to repay him in either her company or with thanks or with sexual favors. I will give compliments only when I am honestly inspired to give them, and usually after already meeting a woman and displaying to her that I'm willing to disagree with her, willing to be rejected by her and willing to walk away from her if it ever comes to that. This willingness to walk away from her and this ability to accept nothing in return is what gives my genuine interest so much value.

When a compliment comes from a man seeking nothing in return, it's a gift of truth, a piece of his vulnerability and infinitely more powerful as a result.

And this honest compliment inspires women to become more highly invested in return. Paradoxically, seeking no investment from her will inspire her to invest that much more in you.

Beautiful women are complimented on their looks often, and 99% of these compliments are given out of neediness, out of some idealization of who she is or what she can do for him.

Beautiful women have been conditioned for most of their lives to know when a man is being genuine or not, whether the compliment is a gift or a bartering tool.

And when it is a gift, when it is honest, she recognizes and appreciates a man who genuinely appreciates her. These men are rare.

Women are people too (radical idea, I know). And as people, we all value those who genuinely value us, not expecting something in return.

The biggest aphrodisiac in the world is someone who likes you, genuinely likes you. A woman's desire is to be desired. But it has to be genuine desire. It can't be a, "I'll desire you as long as you boost my ego and impress my co-workers," kind of desire.

The point is that genuine no-strings-attached appreciation is rare in this world, particularly from men. Women value this and invest themselves in the rare man who can demonstrate his vulnerability to her.

Here's the litmus test. Look at your actions and words around women and look at the intentions behind them. These intentions are always speaking ten times louder than your actual words. What are they saying?

If you bought a girl a drink so that she wouldn't leave to talk to someone else, what does that intention say about you? It says you were over-invested in her and behaving in a manner that was not attractive.

If you told a girl a story in order to impress her and make her like you, what does that intention say about you? It says you were over-invested and behaving in a manner that was not attractive.

If you invited a woman to a restaurant in order to impress her with how much money you had, what does that intention say about you? It says you were over-invested and behaving in a manner that was not attractive.

A man who feels like he needs to buy or steal a woman's attention or affection through entertainment, money or superficiality is a man who is not confident in his identity and who is not genuinely attractive.

I should add that these aren't all-or-nothing propositions either. Look, we all want people to like us, and we all like to impress others. We all need some validation sometimes. We all do these things to certain degrees. It's impossible to be perfectly non-needy all the time.

But neediness is relative. That's why I say it's about being *less invested in others' perceptions* instead of *NOT invested in others' perceptions*. It's an important difference.

I'm not advising to become a heartless sociopath. Quite the opposite, really. Because the more you invest in yourself, the freer you will become to care for others around you without looking for anything in response. A man who is needy and does not invest in himself is ultimately only capable of superficial interactions because his threshold for vulnerability is so low.

It's impossible to be completely devoid of investment in other people. That's how we're wired. But it is always possible to invest and care about yourself more.

Setting Boundaries

But delivering honesty unconditionally isn't just about compliments and appreciation. Unconditional honesty can be brutal and scathing at times as well. And strangely enough, brutal and angry honesty can turn a woman on just as much as the most genuine compliment.

Again, it's not about what's being said, it's about the intention and sub-communication behind it. When you're willing to cut a woman off and tell her when you feel that she's out of line, when you're willing to tell a woman what you will and will not tolerate in your life, this sub-communicates the most powerful elements of attraction to her. Far more powerful than an entertaining story or game.

This is why it's quite possible to piss a woman off and turn her on at the same time. Any man experienced with women will be familiar with this.

If a beautiful woman says something that a needy man finds offensive, he'll ignore it, change the topic, or withhold his true feelings. Hell, he might even pretend to go along with her for fear of making her upset.

But a non-needy man will tell her what she just said was offensive. Let the chips fall where they may. He won't be an asshole about it. He will simply draw a line in the sand, "I don't like stuff like that," and she can choose to step across it or not.

Narcissistic men often misconstrue this as a free ticket to tell people they're always wrong or to basically do what they want without paying attention to the feelings of others.

That's over-compensation and actually the behavior of someone who is over-invested and validated by the reactions of those around him.

A non-needy man *does not* seek to impose himself on the boundaries of others, he's merely interested in maintaining his own boundaries while respecting the boundaries of others.

Non-neediness means you respect yourself AND others. Narcissism means you only respect yourself. Neediness means you only respect others.

The difference is that if a woman says something offensive, a narcissistic man will berate her and try to get her to change her mind, whereas a non-needy man will simply make it clear that he found what she said offensive and will not tolerate it again. How she responds is her choice.

If a woman insults a non-needy man's friends, he will not hesitate to tell her to stop and stand up for those he cares about. If a woman says she needs to leave a date after 30 minutes, he will not try to trick her into staying or beg her to come back, he will not yell at her or lecture her on manners. He will smile and say, "Nice meeting you," and let it go.

Hold your line. Don't go around breaking somebody else's.

Most questions or problems men email me with, at their core, somehow involve a failure to maintain their boundaries. Whether it's about a date, a woman not calling him back, a woman making fun of his job, or whatever, his perceived "problem" is simply him not stepping up and telling her what he's willing to accept and not willing to accept in his relationships.

Typically it has to do with something like the following:

"She really liked me and gave me her number. She responds to my texts, but when I tried to get her out on a date, she made excuses. So then I texted her some more and she said she wanted to see me, but when she did show up for the second date, she was late and said she had to go early. She didn't kiss me. Now I'm texting her and she's texting back but won't agree to go on a third date. What do I do?"

Usually, men like this are obsessive about "the games women play" or how to deal with "tests" from women.

My answer to these men is always the same: if you make it clear from the beginning that you are unwilling to put up with games, then not only will the women you attract stop playing games, but you'll stop attracting women who do.

In the example above, my plan of action? I would have said to her, "Let me know when you'd like to get together again. If you're not interested, that's fine too."

Yes, I will actually say this to her. Not in a harsh manner. But in a clear manner.

I've said something similar to women probably 5-10 times. Without exception, they're completely stunned. Often, they immediately apologize and say that they didn't mean to be so flakey. Oddly enough, my honesty and complete willingness to be rejected (or to reject them) demonstrates my non-neediness and often it causes them to become more attracted to me.

And a couple times, they've said, "You're right. I don't want to date you," in so many words. And that's OK. Yeah, it hurt to hear that. But a lot of shit in life hurts. Get over it. It's for the better. She just saved us both a lot of time and effort.

Your ability and willingness to establish boundaries is inversely proportional to how needy you are. Men who are needy and lack vulnerability will keep their boundaries loose and open, inviting manipulation into their lives and allowing people to walk over them. This is because they are more than willing to alter themselves in order to receive validation from the women they meet.

Men who are non-needy establish strict boundaries because they value their own time and happiness more than receiving attention from a woman. They also see no reason to trample over other people's boundaries.

When it comes to making yourself more vulnerable, the first step is often to begin establishing your own boundaries. Learn how to say no to people, particularly women. Start having opinions on what you like and don't like, what you'll tolerate and won't tolerate. Be honest with yourself, painfully honest. And then be painfully honest with her.

The problem with forming strong boundaries is that in order to form them, you have to be particularly aware of your own desires and emotions. And many men who have been needy their entire lives are not very self-aware. They don't know what they're willing to stand up for and what they're willing to let slide. They don't know their own emotional motivations and desires.

Men will often have to spend a lot of time seeking truth within themselves first before they're able to express it to others.

Finding Your Truth

Here are some truths that I've found out about myself:

My overwhelming desire for affection from women probably has a lot to do with the fact that I was raised by a single mom in adolescence. My parents' divorce left a deep-seated fear of commitment in me that permeated all of my relationships into my 30s. That a lot of what I considered cool when I was younger was really just different ways to protect myself and medicate my emotional wounds. That I resented my dad for a long time. That I have a peculiar obsession with my masculinity. That my most important values are honesty, empathy, and intellectual curiosity. That I'm unwilling to tolerate women who don't make me happy, no matter how hot they are.

It's easy for me to say these things now, and what's important is not the words. What's important is the floodgates of emotions that came up as I discovered these truths about myself. As I discovered these things about myself, it allowed me to express previously stifled emotions in my daily life and with women.

Because as I've discovered each one of the above truths about myself, I've then been able to draw boundaries based on that truth, which in turn makes me less needy.

For instance, when I first started going out, I spent a lot of time beating my head against a wall trying to pick up the "hot" club girls at loud nightclubs. You know, fake tans, fake tits, fake hair, fake personalities.

For whatever reason, I couldn't keep their attention long enough. Eventually, after pushing things further and spending more time and effort in those places than I care to admit, I went home with a few of them.

And... well, it was pretty disappointing.

What I discovered is that there was not anything objectively better or more interesting about these girls. The only thing that seems to attract men to them is the fact that they look like women they see on TV and movies and in porn. There's nothing genuinely enticing about them other than that they are seen as a status symbol. And chasing them was borne out of neediness, not genuine honesty. It took me a couple years, but I eventually realized that I was chasing a status symbol, a pat on the back, basically reliving and redeeming all of my failed high school moments where the pretty girls didn't pay attention to me.

It had nothing to do with the women; it had everything to do with me.

Now, when I meet a woman at a place like that who doesn't show me any depth to her personality, I'm unwilling to put any more effort into getting to know her. My boundary is established: I value curiosity, education, intelligence and authenticity. I also don't value "fake" looks such as pounds of make-up, bronzer, hair extensions or super tight skirts.

OK, maybe I do value the tight skirts.

But the irony? Because that boundary is established, I'm not invested in these women much at all, and as a result, I get more attention from them than ever before.

It's important to look at the reasons why you're over-invested around women and have an honest discussion with yourself about it to try and resolve it.

For instance, perhaps you're over-invested around women because you're a virgin and have no experience with them. Then you need to look at how being inexperienced is causing you to undervalue yourself and seek validation. You must become comfortable with the idea of being inexperienced and be comfortable admitting that insecurity if you wish to gain a lot of experience.

Or perhaps your ex-girlfriend left you for another man and you're bitter. Before you can undo the anger that is causing you to be over-invested, you need to come to terms with why you're angry and accept why your ex left you.

For me, a big part of this was accepting that, actually, I had been a pretty naive and shitty boyfriend to my ex-girlfriend and I could understand why she would want to leave me. I also recognized flaws and insecurities in her that I hadn't noticed when we were together and that she hadn't been the perfect angel that I assumed she was. All in all, I came to terms with the experience and the anger receded, allowing me to let go and become less invested in women I dated.

Another example is a guy who has never been "cool" before. Perhaps he was picked on growing up and made fun of all through high school. Maybe the popular guys in school told him he was gay and a pussy.

Perhaps now he's older, better looking and more social and is looking to compensate for all of those years of feeling insignificant. So he does it by throwing money around and attracting a lot of superficial attention. He's having fun, but he's scratching that itch, he's finally living out that need to be the cool and popular guy. But at some point, he has to come to terms with this, accept it, and become comfortable admitting it. Then he can move on.

Again, if you're only trying to get women to impress other guys, then you're not in a very good place, and you need to take a serious look at your motivations. To undo this, you must come to terms with why you're seeking attention and approval from other men — maybe it goes as far back as your father — and then seek to find that approval through other means. Join a sports team. Take your co-workers out for beers. Buy season tickets to the local basketball team. There are much healthier ways to get male camaraderie than to try and impress other guys by getting girls.

For me, I had a combination of the second two examples. I spent most of my adolescence living alone with my mother. As a result, I always related more to girls than to boys, and had few male friends until I reached adulthood. I never could relate to them as well, and not having my father around as much (both physically and emotionally) drove me to unconsciously seek a lot of approval from other men.

Throw on top of that the fact my girlfriend of four years left me, and I had a lot of anger toward women. Combine the two and you have a perfect recipe for a needy man who turned to narcissism in order to over-compensate and become a player.

Recognizing and accepting these truths is the only thing that allowed me to resolve and let go of a lot of my investment and neediness toward women's approval. I had to come to terms with these faults within myself before I could finally attract amazing women into my life with consistency. As soon as my need to impress other men dissipated, so did my investment in how a drunken girl in a bar thought of me. As soon as I let go of some of my anger towards my ex, some of my need to fuck absolutely everything disappeared too.

As a result, I became less invested and less affected by the actions of the women around me, which in turn made me more attractive around them. As if by magic, I began to attract far more beautiful and interesting women with less effort.

And how do I know this? It was clear. My looks didn't change. I dressed the same way. Went to the same parties and bars. But suddenly women were approaching me. I was catching more beautiful women smiling at me and staring at me. My outward appearance had changed little. My inner disposition changed entirely. My outward behaviors soon followed suit.

Seeking the truth within yourself is a long-term progress. An entire book could be written on it by itself. But I guarantee that you have some deep-seated truths that are currently causing you to invest too heavily in how women treat you. Otherwise, you wouldn't have bought this book or read this far.

If you feel like you have some serious emotional issues or believe that for whatever reason you're basing an insanely high amount of your identity on how women respond to you, then I recommend therapy.

Therapy has a lot of negative stereotypes and judgments that come along with it, but if you take the time to find a good therapist who you trust and gel with, then it can be extremely helpful.

The important thing about therapy is to remember that it's a tool, not a solution. A therapist is there to guide you and motivate you in continuing to find your own emotional truths about yourself. He or she can't find them for you. A lot of people show up to therapy expecting a therapist to magically fix them. They then get frustrated when all they do is "talk" and get asked annoying questions the whole session.

Those questions are asked for a reason. Be pro-active in finding the emotional knots in yourself that you didn't know were there before. You'll discover some amazing things. That time the neighbor's kids locked you in a closet all afternoon, or the time your mother went home and forgot you at the grocery store, or a parent's divorce or death of a loved one — these all have emotional repercussions that can and probably will motivate you and drive you to over-invest in receiving validation from one specific source or another in your life.

And that source is sometimes women.

Following the advice of this book should help as well. All the advice in the book is crafted to help you develop non-neediness. Implementing these behaviors and becoming more aware of your emotions while you're doing them should help you down the road to permanent change.

As you'll see, the book is divided up into three core areas: building a congruent and attractive lifestyle for yourself, overcoming your fears and anxieties, and becoming socially adept at expressing your emotions and sexuality without shame or hesitation.

All three of these sections will help you become more vulnerable and less needy. As we'll talk about in Chapter 6, these things are all interconnected. When you work on one of them, you indirectly benefit the others, and vice-versa.

Friction and Projection

I'd like to finish up the chapter discussing a couple of exceptions when it comes to being vulnerable and non-needy around women. I know at the beginning of the book I made the promise that being less invested in any particular woman than she is invested in you will make her perceive you as attractive.

Well, that's true, but just because she perceives you as an attractive man, doesn't mean she'll immediately want to jump into bed with you.

Attraction is great, but in and of itself, it's not always enough to consummate a romantic or sexual relationship.

There are two main reasons that prevent attracted women from being with you, and they are both quite common: I call them friction and projection.

Friction is when a woman finds you to be an attractive man, but there are value differences or external circumstances that prevent her from acting on that attraction or being interested in you.

For instance, let's say you're a rock star who spends his nights getting drunk and banging groupies and she's a born-again Christian and has sworn off all sex before marriage. That mismatch in personal values is going to disrupt any potential of ever being together and is a genuine piece of friction that is going to prevent anything from happening.

The most common case is the girlfriend/wife. This happens all the time. You meet a woman, you two really click, she's laughing at all your jokes, smiles when you smile, looks into your eyes a little bit too long...

...and she's married.

And not only is she married but she makes a point to cut the flirting off before it goes too far. She likes you. She may even say that she's attracted to you and be honest. But she values her marriage more than her attraction to you. And there's nothing you can do about that. That's friction.

Men often used to ask me how to get a woman to cheat on her boyfriend or husband. My answer has two parts. The first part is: you don't, they decide. The second part of the answer is: don't fucking do it, what's wrong with you? It contributes to the fucking of people's lives and even if it didn't, it's never worth the headache it causes.

Friction can be religious, cultural or simply due to poor logistics. For instance, some legit friction would be if she lives in Australia and you live in New York. That creates some problems for dating despite strong attraction.

There's usually at least a little bit of friction in any interaction. You're never going to like 100% of any woman and no woman is ever going to like 100% of you. There will be slight differences in values or priorities that will irk you just a little bit, or maybe a lot. There will also be unavoidable situations and events that will cause obstacles to you two being together.

Whether this friction prevents a sexual relationship from occurring though will depend on the strength of your boundaries and what your expectations are.

For instance, you may meet a really hot girl who is a cocaine addict. But if you kind of just want to have sex with her, you may overlook the cocaine addiction. Then again, if you have a major moral issue with narcotics, then you'll probably be turned off and pass up on her.

Ultimately, your values determine your behavior. And that's kind of the point of all of this: YOUR values determine your behavior, not what you think she wants, not what you think others want, but what is best for you and best for the relationship.

Projection is completely different. There are a lot of women who, for whatever reason, are afraid of their own sexuality and/or openly sexual men. They harbor trust issues and resentment with men. Usually, this is because they have a history of some sort of emotional/sexual abuse and/or they've experienced a long string of disappointments with the men in their life.

When confronted with a non-needy man — a man *without* these similar emotional hang-ups and distrust — these women will usually be untrusting and lash out in response. They are not lashing out for lack of attraction, but they are lashing out *because* they are attracted and that strong sexual attraction scares them, particularly if you're a man who feels threatening to them. Their view of male sexuality is negative and when they are confronted with an honest and attractive man they'll often attack you and try to tear you down for it.

These are the women who will get angry and say snide things like, "I bet you say that to all the girls," or will find reasons to push you away and then regret it and want you back. They will pretend to miss your calls and then get angry when you don't persist in calling them, or they'll make up excuses to ignore you on a date and then get mad when you don't behave like a gentleman.

Needless to say, you're better off without these women. Take the rejection and move on.

Generally, these women are extremely needy, and because of the large investment gap between you two, they will try to project their own investment onto you. They will accuse you of being demanding, overbearing, too horny, untrustworthy, or weak. These accusations will have little to no connection to reality, and a non-needy man will either walk away from a girl like this or simply ignore her accusations if they have no bearing.

The only men willing to put up with such nonsense are men who are highly needy as well. The needy man will spend all of his time placating and trying to fix the accusations and problems the woman projects onto him. And the most messed up part about this is that the needy man will *enjoy fixing and placating the needy woman*. The needy man enjoys it because this constant "fixing" of the distrusting woman's fears and accusations makes the needy man feel needed.

If the man is narcissistic, then he will usually lash out right back at the woman and they will engage in a relationship full of petty, unimportant drama, playing out emotions and projecting their histories of pain and marginalization onto each other over and over again, until one of them finally becomes conscious enough to break the cycle and move on. Sometimes this happens quickly. Other times it takes months or years. Either way, it's always unpleasant.

The uncomfortable truth is that the majority of women are going to have high degrees of friction and projection when you meet them. With most of the women you meet, things are simply not going to work no matter what you do or say. This is to be expected. And this is fine. You are going to be incompatible with most of the women in the world and to hold any hopes of being highly compatible with most is an illusion of grandeur and a figment of your own narcissistic tendency.

Incompatibility is a fact of life. No matter how you behave or what you're into, the majority of women out there at any given time are simply not going to be interested or emotionally available to you. Our job is not to attract every woman, but to screen for women with a high potential of being attracted to who we really are.

The reality of incompatibility defines our entire strategy of dating women. To base our strategy on anything else is inefficient at best and downright damaging at worst. The world is what it is, it's our job to simply present ourselves as boldly and clearly to it as possible, accept the reactions and move on the opportunities. Any attempt to control the reactions of others or take some kind of power over the reactions you receive is both foolish and illusory.

Part II: Strategy

Chapter 4
Polarization

In Part I, we learned that male attractiveness is based on how non-needy one is and how comfortable one is in expressing one's desire and vulnerability. We also learned the limitations of attraction and how most of the women in the world at any given time are not going to be compatible with you no matter what you say or do.

In Part II, our goal is to create a real world strategy based on these realities so that any man can map out a clear way to improve his dating life quickly and drastically.

The goals of this strategy are efficacy and practicality. This is a strategy based on *reality*, not based on some sort of mythology about unlocking the secrets of every woman, or lofty promises to be able to sleep with every single hot girl you ever meet.

As a result, the strategy in this book deals with realities that a lot of other men's dating advice does not deal with; namely, rejection, race, age, appearance, shame, honesty, emotional connection and did I mention rejection?

You will get rejected. But don't worry. It's a good thing.

A lot of dating advice, particularly of the performance variety, tries to promise the ability to have sex with any girl you want, regardless of... well, pretty much anything. You could be a fat slob living in your mother's basement, and with the right two or three lines, you too can date a lingerie model (as if there's a lingerie model hanging out on every street corner).

This is a fairy tale. And not only is it a fairy tale, it's a fairy tale you don't actually want to live. It feeds your neediness.

Rejection exists for a reason — it's a means to keep people apart who are not good for each other.

Men don't seem to understand that if a woman rejects him because he's short, or because she doesn't like his hair, or because she finds him boring, then he wasn't going to enjoy being around her anyway.

Ask yourself this: why would you want to be intimate with someone who doesn't appreciate you? Why would you *ever* settle for such a person? Because she's hot? Come on, have a little more self-respect. Have some higher standards.

Again, the men who are needy and have poor self-esteem are the ones who are willing to completely alter their personalities in order to seduce *any* woman. The first step to being more attractive is to see rejection as a means to eliminate women who won't make you happy from your life. It's a blessing, not a curse.

So let's start at the beginning. There are an infinite number of women out there, and we can't possibly meet or even know all of them. So our first task is to find a way to narrow them down and screen them in a way that we can manage our opportunities better.

The Three Categories of Women

Let's start with all of the women on the planet. That's something like 3.6 billion or so.

Obviously, you are not going to desire the majority of the women in the world. So we can cross out all of the ones who are physically not to your taste. If you don't find a woman attractive, don't hit on her, don't ask her out, don't do anything.

That said, decide whatever you like in a woman by your own standards. If you like big girls or curvy girls, go for it. If you prefer black girls with dreadlocks, more power to you. If you like older women or younger women, cool. Don't pressure yourself to live up to someone else's standards. And again, for the love of god, *if you don't find her attractive, don't pursue her.*

For practical purposes, we can divide up all of the women you're attracted to into three categories: Receptive, Neutral and Unreceptive.

Let's start with Unreceptive.

Women who are Unreceptive are just that: they're unavailable and/or uninterested in having a sexual/romantic relationship with you. The most common reasons that put women in this category are the following:

- You're far needier than she is, and she's therefore not attracted to you.
- She has a boyfriend/husband and is happy in her relationship.
- There's too much friction preventing her from being willing to date you, such as a difference in values, difference in interests, bad logistics, etc.
- She's not interested or looking for *any* man at the moment.

The way to tell if a woman is Unreceptive is if she repeatedly does not reciprocate your signs of interest and/or shows you signs of disinterest. If you invite her out for coffee and she keeps making excuses to why she can't, then she's Unreceptive. If you call her three times and she never calls back, then she is Unreceptive. If you chat her up and she explains that she is busy and wants to be alone, then she is Unreceptive. If you hang out with her and she talks about how frustrated she is with her boyfriend and how you're such a good listener, then she's Unreceptive.

No exceptions. Many men waste a lot of time convincing themselves that Unreceptive women may actually like them. A good rule of thumb here is, "if you have to ask, then that's your answer." That is, there should be no ambiguity here. And if there is, you can quickly solve it by simply stating to her, "I think you're cute/pretty/attractive/funny/whatever, want to grab coffee/dinner/a drink sometime?"

Problem solved. You'll find out where you are very quickly.

But I'm getting ahead of myself…

The next category is Neutral. This category can be difficult for men to understand because it's not as common for us as it is for women. Typically, a man knows within a few seconds if he's willing to meet and even sleep with a woman or not.

Women aren't like that. They spend a lot of time being unsure about a man and need to be swayed one way or the other.

Women in this category are usually women who you've just met or have only spent a little bit of time with. The important thing to know is that women do not ever *stay* in this category. They eventually polarize one way or the other. And if you never make an advance or show interest in them, then they will *usually* polarize towards being Unreceptive (this is the Friend Zone, which we'll cover in a minute).

Neutral women are generally just that, neutral. They will not necessarily turn down your offers, but they won't offer or reciprocate themselves. The jury's still out. They'll often tentatively say yes, although they won't seem overly enthusiastic about it. They're still testing the waters. Or sometimes, they just haven't considered you in that way yet.

The goal with Neutral women is to polarize them through your words and behaviors. This may mean flirting with them or teasing them. It may mean asking her on a date. It may be as simple as smiling at her from across the room. Whatever it is, the goal with Neutral women is to take an action that forces her to make a decision about how she feels about you. Which side she polarizes to is far less important than actually taking action. And remember, if you leave her to her neutrality, she will *usually* become Unreceptive and not see you as dating material.

And in the final category, women who are Receptive are women who are sexually/romantically attracted to you. You can recognize women who are Receptive in two ways: 1) they initiate with you, and/or 2) they reciprocate your actions enthusiastically.

Some examples of a woman initiating with you:

- She makes strong eye contact with you and doesn't break it.
- She approaches you.
- She touches you unprovoked.
- She asks for your number or invites you out with her/her friends.
- She asks you a lot of questions about yourself and seems genuinely interested in you.
- She introduces you to her friends.
- She gives you her number.
- She comes up with some excuse/story/reason for you to hang out with her or spend time with her.

Chances are if you're reading this book, many of the girlfriends or sexual experiences you've had with women in the past only happened because she initiated with you.

That's fine. But just going about your life, unless you are extremely good-looking or have a great lifestyle or you manage to meet women through good social contacts, few women are going to initiate with you and the few who do won't initiate often.

In fact, most women, especially very beautiful women, even if they're attracted to you, won't initiate with you. Remember, women tend to be less invested before sex, therefore, they (usually) expect men to initiate in the beginning. There are also strong cultural pressures on women to wait for the man to initiate.

The other way women demonstrate that they're Receptive is when they reciprocate. It's important to recognize the subtle difference between a woman reciprocating your advances and a woman being neutral toward your advances. A woman who is Neutral will simply not respond at all. For instance, if you touch a Neutral woman on her back while you speak to her, she'll just act like you're not touching her.

A woman who is reciprocating will do something to respond positively to your advance. Think of it as her signaling to you that she accepts your advancing on her and likes it. If you touched a woman on the back and she wanted to reciprocate, she would either lean back into you, lean in closer to you, or touch you in return.

Here are some other common examples of reciprocation:

- She ignores her friends to stay and talk to you.
- She keeps very strong eye contact and laughs a little too much at everything you say.
- When you touch her, she touches you in return.
- When you put your arm around her, she leans into you.
- When you take her hand to move somewhere, she holds it in return.
- When you ask her out on a date, she offers a place to go or mentions something she'd like to do with you.

Most interested women will reciprocate on small signals to show that they're interested in you. Catching on to how women reciprocate and noticing the signals is something that you develop with experience, but it shouldn't be too hard if you know what to pay attention to.

A lot of the methods of flirting that we'll cover in Part V will address the specific ways in which women reciprocate and how to handle them.

Unfortunately, the vast majority of women you will meet, assuming you're a typical guy, will be either Neutral or Unreceptive. This is true for the most of the male population, myself included, so don't worry.

The percentage of women that you meet in each category will vary widely from man to man and also vary widely depending on the context in which you meet women.

For instance, you could be a 40-year-old investing mogul, and at networking events or conferences, you may find that 40% or more women are Receptive and few make themselves Unreceptive or Neutral.

But that same man can go to a nightclub full of drunken 20-year-olds and soon find that only 1% of women are Receptive or Neutral, and 99% are Unreceptive.

This is a concept I call *Demographics*, and I've devoted all of Chapter 7 to it because it's extremely important.

The exact percentages of women falling into each category aren't really that relevant. A lot of men, and even a lot of dating advice books, misplace a lot of time and effort due to not understanding these three categories and the strategies that go along with them.

Strategies for Each Category

Your course of action will differ depending on the type of woman you meet. Many men make the mistake of applying the wrong strategy to the wrong category of women. For instance, they'll try to convince an Unreceptive woman to become Receptive. Or they'll treat a woman who's already Receptive as if she isn't yet. Not only is this a time waster, it's also ineffective.

The goal with Unreceptive women is to identify them and move on as quickly as possible. They're time sinks. Typically, if women are Unreceptive, they're Unreceptive for a good reason, and it has little to do with you (or maybe it does has everything to do with you, in which case you should learn from it).

You're almost never going to change the mind of an Unreceptive woman, and even when you do it's often not worth the effort.

I strongly believe in the idea of "Fuck Yes or No." That is, I want women to say "Fuck Yes," once they've gotten to know me. And if they aren't enthusiastic and excited about being with me, then I'm not interested in them anymore. So Unreceptive women simply aren't worth my time or effort to pursue. They could be great people and maybe I'll be friends with them. But the minute they're Unreceptive towards me, my interests have moved on.

I'll say this: in seven years, after meeting thousands of women, I can think of maybe five instances where a woman was flat out Unreceptive towards me and I "won her over." If she shuts you down, tells you to go away, tells you she's not interested, tells you she has a boyfriend, move on. Seriously, get over it and move on. You're wasting your time. I don't care how special you think she is, there's another one out there who's just as special who *will be* Receptive to you.

The two most common time sinks with Unreceptive Women are the Friend Zone and women in relationships.

The Friend Zone occurs when a woman has categorized you as a friend and not a potential lover. For women, these categories are almost always mutually exclusive. A man is either a friend, or a potential sexual partner, but rarely both. There are exceptions, but they are rare.

Once inside of it, the Friend Zone is almost impossible to get out. And if you do ever get out, it's likely not due to anything you tried or did anyway. Why? Because a man who does not act on his sexual desires is a man who is needy, lacks vulnerability and is therefore unattractive.

The Friend Zone typically occurs when a man meets a Receptive or Neutral woman but never makes a move or expresses his interest. Instead, he behaves pleasantly, like a good friend would. In his mind, this is great because it means she likes talking to him, laughs at his jokes, etc. But because he's withholding his sexual interest, he's placing himself in her mind firmly in the "friend" camp.

A classic, yet painful example of the Friend Zone happened with a friend of my ex-girlfriend. When I met her, she was moving into her new apartment. There were two guys helping her move in. One was a tall fellow who obviously seemed eager to please her and help as much as he could. It did not take long to recognize that he was quite needy around her and made poor attempts to flirt, which she did not reciprocate.

71

She, of course, being an attractive girl, was not highly invested back, and so I immediately pegged him as in her Friend Zone. As it turned out, I was right.

This guy hated me the whole time I dated her. He was convinced that I was an asshole because he had been so nice to her for so long, and I came along and simply asked her out without giving a shit whether she said yes or not. Funny how that works. A couple years later, after she and I broke up and remained friends, he refused to let her talk about me around him. During this period, he made numerous attempts to get with her, sometimes going as far as making tearful proclamations that he had been in love with her for years.

Needless to say, all of these attempts turned her off and she shut down. It ruined the friendship. They had been friends with each other for over four years, and the degree of investment he was showing, even despite his behavior (the fact that he spent four years working up the nerve to make a move) sub-communicated a *massive* degree of neediness and horrible self-worth.

Obviously, she rejected him. Again and again, she rejected him. So he became angry. And perceiving me to have been an asshole who didn't treat her well, he decided to try to be an asshole who didn't treat her well either. He went down the road of narcissism and overcompensation. He began to behave disrespectfully towards her, believing that she must have no self-respect if she rejected men who treated her so well like he did. And in a growing irony, feeling entitled due to how "nice" he had been for years, he felt as though he deserved to treat her worse and objectify her, to the point where one night he physically tried to force her to kiss him.

Needless to say, the friendship was over, as she refused to ever see him again.

The Friend Zone is the biggest possible time sink because most men who are stuck in it entertain fantasies that they're simply waiting for the inevitable to occur. It plays into their fantasies of romance and destiny. Their perspective is that *they* are the perfect man for her and one day when *she* wakes up and realizes how foolish she is, she'll realize that the love of her life had been sitting right there by her side all along.

This never happens. Ever. It's an incredibly arrogant and manipulative mindset to adopt. It's no wonder women see it as so unattractive.

If you are in this situation now, you need to get it out of your head and move on. Immediately. Typically, if men have been friends with a woman for even a month or two without ever explicitly indicating their sexual interest in her, it's likely too late.

You must indicate some sort of sexual interest early on. Otherwise, the longer you wait, the harder it gets and the more likely she will become Unreceptive to you. Again, ask yourself what waiting four years to state your interest in a girl sub-communicates to her. It sub-communicates, "I am so much more invested in you than in myself that I spent four years working up the nerve to show you my interest." It's extremely unattractive. And chances are, she's knows! She always knew! Which just makes it worse.

The second time sink that men often get sucked into is a woman that is happily in a relationship. Unlike the Friend Zone where men will often waste away months or years, a woman in a relationship will usually only waste a few weeks, maybe a few months at the most. But still, a time sink is a time sink.

A lot of men get hung up on women who are already taken, and rather than cut their losses and move on, they harbor some fantasy that any woman will cheat on her boyfriend/husband given the right circumstance. This isn't true. And even in the cases that it is true, it's also not worth the time or effort.

Waiting around for a woman in a relationship is simply not worth it. Period. Trying to sabotage a woman's relationship so you can swoop in and "steal" her is not only ineffectual but morally fucked up. It's neediness and narcissism to an extreme degree.

What a lot of men *don't* understand though is that oftentimes, married or taken women will still flirt with other men for no other reason than they think it's fun and they like the attention. To some women, flirting is like a hobby and they see it as harmless fun. If a woman is married or has a boyfriend and seems pretty happy in general and is flirting with me, then I don't take the flirting too seriously.

Men also struggle a lot with the rejection, "I have a boyfriend." Some men seem to get obsessed about whether this is actually true or she's just saying it to reject him.

Once again, it's not about whether her statement is factual or not. It's about her intention. The intention is, "I'm not interested."

Take *that* at face value and move on. Even if she doesn't have a boyfriend, there's no point in trying to win over a girl who is willing to lie about something like that to you. And if she does have a boyfriend, then she's probably happy with him, otherwise, she wouldn't have brought it up.

And that's really the crux of the matter: women who have boyfriends/husbands who are willing to cheat on them, don't bring up their boyfriends/husbands... almost ever. Typically, you'll hear about them either immediately before or immediately after you hook up with them. If they tell you about them right when you meet them, then they're not interested. If they tell you about their boyfriend while they're making out with you in the cab back to your apartment, then she's probably interested. But you don't need me to tell you that.

So your mission with Unreceptive women is to spot them as quickly as possible, and then politely move on. Rejection, in this case, is often your friend, as we'll see later.

It's not until you find a woman who is Neutral or better that things begin to get interesting.

The goal with Neutral Women is to get them to stop being Neutral as soon as possible. As we mentioned earlier, women who are Neutral and who stay Neutral tend to eventually end up Unreceptive. You do this by expressing your vulnerability and your identity to them freely.

When you express your truth to women, you will polarize them — they will either become Receptive to you or they will make themselves Unreceptive. When you express your truth, if you express more investment than them, then they will be not be attracted to you and will therefore be Unreceptive. Also, if you express your truth and there is a high amount of friction between you and her that cannot be overcome, then she will become Unreceptive

If you express your truth and demonstrate not only that you're non-needy but also frictionless for her (similar interests, values, life situation, etc.), then she will become very Receptive. And when I say very Receptive, I mean very.

A big misconception men have is that they think they need to behave in a way that makes every single woman like them – as if women were all the same. This is counterproductive because by altering your behavior to fit whatever she wants, it means you are not being vulnerable and, therefore, you are being needy and unattractive.

Other men often stick to plain jokes and safe topics of conversation that end up not polarizing at all for fear of being rejected. This is also a form of hiding one's truth, not showing vulnerability, being over-invested and therefore not attractive.

This is the plight of the highly needy "Nice Guy." He's afraid of eliciting an emotional response in anybody, especially women (and especially himself); therefore, he'll play it safe and elicit Neutral reactions from woman after woman. And when women are Neutral for too long without being polarized, then they will make themselves Unreceptive.

If there is one thing that narcissistic men accomplish well, it's that they will polarize women quickly. Women will know more or less immediately if they're interested in a narcissistic guy or not because he will be so overbearing and imposing she'll have no choice other than to feel something for him.

The problem with the narcissistic man is that the few women who become Receptive to him are not the type of women who are pleasant to be around (as they're highly needy themselves).

As you can see, Neutral women are where so-called "game" comes into play. Having good game means you can take a woman who is Neutral and incite her to become Receptive to you quickly. You do this by making yourself vulnerable, sharing yourself unabashedly, and polarizing her one way or the other and being comfortable with either result.

For instance, I recently met a beautiful woman in a nightclub. She danced with me but ignored my attempts to get closer to her. She seemed content to dance with me but was not investing any effort in the interaction beyond that. Sensing that I could easily get stuck dancing with her all night without actually polarizing her, I asked that we go get a drink. I told her I'd like to get to know her a bit better and talk. She obliged.

At the bar, the first question out of my mouth is one of my favorites for Neutral situations: "What's your favorite thing in the world?"

This question will tell me two things: how passionate and self-aware she is about her own life, and secondly if we have anything in common. Women who are not passionate or self-aware I drop very quickly and go meet someone else. Women who share interests with me give me an opportunity to polarize them quickly to being Receptive.

For instance, if a woman answers "Jesus," then I know I'm heading straight for Unreceptive right then and there. Not that I hate Jesus or anything, but let's just say there's a conflict of interests. This polarization is a good thing, though, even though it ends up with me not getting the girl in the end. We're both better off not being together. And by me eliciting her religiosity early on, we find that out sooner rather than later.

In this particular example at the nightclub, the woman answered traveling and experiencing new cultures. Bingo. I love to travel. I've been to over 40 countries. I tell her this. Sure enough, within 30 minutes, we were sitting alone together, enrapt in a conversation about grammar and the Russian language.

Do Russian grammar lessons strike you as an effective pick up tactic? Probably not. But I dig it. And so did she. And she eventually became my girlfriend. My success was about expressing my identity, forcing her to make a decision about me and letting the chips fall where they may.

Finally, we have the Receptive women. Finding these are the best because they are the most rewarding interactions while requiring the least amount of effort. When you meet a Receptive woman, the goal is simple. You escalate. You make a move. You move things forward — assuming you want to, of course.

Receptive women who were originally Neutral, if you do not make a move and become physical with them quickly enough, they will often drift back to Neutral and then to Unreceptive permanently. But I've found that women who are Receptive to you to begin with will usually stay Receptive almost indefinitely. I think these are the only rare occasions when you can actually pry yourself out of the Friend Zone — these rare circumstances where she was always Receptive to you, but for whatever reason, you two weren't able to be together (you had a girlfriend, she moved away for three years, etc.).

The percentage of women who are Receptive to you will increase proportionally to the quality of your lifestyle, your social status, and your looks. The percentage of women that you're able to move from Neutral to Receptive will be proportional to how good your "game" is, or how well you're able to communicate and express yourself with women. And your ability to sort through each type of women and meet as many as possible will be determined by how fearless and bold you are when it comes to meeting women.

(That last paragraph was important and the basis for the rest of this book, so you may want to read it again and make sure you understand it.)

While most pick up advice obsesses over the avoidance of rejection, rejection plays an integral part in my strategy. It's unavoidable, so I figure we may as well develop a strategy that uses it to help us. Rejection exists for a reason. If you are a professor at a prestigious university, then you're probably not going to enjoy your time with a high school dropout with an alcohol problem. Just because she has a nice ass doesn't mean you want to be with her.

Polarizing women into rejecting us — and when I say us, I mean the *real* us, the vulnerable and unabashed us — does us a favor by sorting out which women are going to make us happy.

Men often want to have it both ways — they want to be able to avoid painful rejections, avoid saying something stupid, avoid embarrassing themselves, while at the same time being this attractive, amazing guy who women fall to their knees for.

You can't have it both ways.

The two go together. You *cannot* be an attractive and life-changing presence to some women without being a joke or an embarrassment to others. You simply can't. You have to be controversial. You have to polarize. It's the name of the game. And getting good at the game is learning to open yourself up enough emotionally, learning to express your honest self enough and be comfortable enough with your vulnerability to take those embarrassing moments along with the moments of passion. A willingness to polarize is not easy. But it's necessary. It's why you're here right now.

Polarizing to Attract

Our primary strategy with women is polarization. The idea is that the more forthright you are about who you are, how you feel, and what you think, the more this is going to weed out Unreceptive Women from the

Receptive women, as well as push Neutral women to get off the fence and decide how they feel about you.

The amazing thing about polarization is that the simple act of doing it demonstrates non-neediness and will then inspire more Neutral women to become Receptive than other strategies or tactics.

Like I mentioned earlier, the most common strategy by men who are inexperienced with women is "to be liked by all, hated by none." But when it comes to being intimate and attracting women, this is a horrible strategy. Being hated by nobody usually means you're not loved by anybody either.

The men who employ this strategy employ it because they're trying to avoid confrontation and controversy. Many of these men have been avoiding confrontation and controversy their entire lives. It's part of their fear of vulnerability.

The fact is that sexuality, attraction, and relationships are, by their very nature, confrontational and controversial. You have to either make the decision to accept being controversial and confrontational or you need to accept that you will go through life with everyone being Neutral towards you.

Polarization is what occurs when you express your truth and make yourself vulnerable. When you tell a woman she is beautiful, you are polarizing her. When you tease her about her earrings and put your arm around her, you're polarizing her. When you wear a custom-made suit when you go out, you are polarizing women. When you tell a woman who's late to a date to never be late again, you are polarizing her. When you smile and tell her how beautiful she is, you're polarizing her. When you take her hand in yours and lead her somewhere, you are polarizing her.

Everything that is attractive is polarizing.

These are never wrong moves, assuming that they are *honest* expressions of yourself and you are showing your vulnerability.

A man who is highly invested is going to alter his behaviors based on the woman he's talking to. He's going to be afraid to tell her that he doesn't accept her being late. He's going to be afraid to wear that suit out. He's going to be timid when he wants to put his arm around her. He's going to be unable to make himself vulnerable, express his truth, and will therefore not polarize her.

A man who is uninhibited about expressing his emotions and what he wants will demonstrate non-neediness, thereby attracting a woman and immediately forcing her to decide whether she's Receptive or Unreceptive. And chances are, unless there's a lot of friction present, she will become Receptive. You'd be surprised how many women will respond with attraction to nothing other than a man who is bold and willing to stick his neck out.

A lot of men assume that this means you are inviting a mountain of rejection onto you. The surprising thing is this is rarely the case. Yes, you will get rejected when you polarize women. And yes, every once in a while it will be a harsh rejection.

But surprisingly, *a lot* of women will react warmly to these advances, even if they're not interested and reject you. They respect a man who is bold and honest. I've had tons occasions where I approached women boldly and honestly, stating directly that they were beautiful and I wanted to meet them, and despite rejecting me, they were so impressed by my boldness and confidence that they promptly introduced me to a friend of theirs who was available.

I've often been thanked by the women who I've unsuccessfully hit on, not because I did it, but *for the way I did it*. And even when things go nowhere, women at least respect me and the fact that I bluntly state what I feel.

Most of the harsh rejections I've had in my life came from when I was performing, seeking validation, when I was over-invested and needy and overcompensating. When I pursue women in a vulnerable way, almost every woman at the very least will respect my advances, even if she's not interested.

In my experience, the more polarizing a man is, the more they are flooded with opportunities with women. This is true for every man I know who is incredibly successful with meeting and dating women.

The biggest mental hurdle for many men is the ability to handle rejection. A lot of men have had it ingrained into them all of their lives — and even by other dating advice — that rejection is terrible and should be avoided at all costs. They buy into some myth that there are magical lady's men out there that don't get rejected, ever.

And as we'll see, this is not true.

Chapter 5
Rejection and Success

Business guru Dan Kennedy once said, "Your ability to deal with the failure will determine how much you get to deal with success."

My harshest rejection ever was in Austin, Texas, probably winter of 2007. I was out with my best friend late on a Friday night. I see two cute girls dancing by themselves. I approach. I lightly touch one on the shoulder and begin to speak.

She spins around, "GET THE FUCK AWAY FROM ME! DON'T YOU EVER FUCKING TOUCH ME!"

"Whoa, chill out, I didn't do anything!" I try to blurt out between her shrieks. I'm not heard. She shoves me backward while screaming at me. I push her arms back to protect myself.

The slap comes hard and fast. Totally uncalled for. "GET THE FUCK AWAY FROM ME! DON'T YOU EVER FUCKING TOUCH ME AGAIN!"

Before I know it bouncers are removing me from the bar.

"I didn't even do anything, I don't even know her," I say.

"Yeah, whatever buddy," the bouncer says. I get outside and my friend comes out to meet me. "Dude, what fucked up thing did you say now?"

"I didn't say *anything.*" He looks at me skeptically. "No, seriously, I didn't say anything."

"Yeah, whatever."

Another night, another bar. This was probably sometime in 2006. I'm talking to a super cute blonde. College girl. Sorority. Ditsy as hell and a true pain to interact with. You know those people who interrupt you constantly and redirect every possible topic of conversation back to some inane story about themselves? She was one of those. It was like being socially waterboarded.

But she was hot. And I was young and needy and crazy horny and honestly had nothing better to do. So I talked to her, painfully and begrudgingly.

Somewhere in between trying to decide whether to drown myself in alcohol, to drown her in alcohol, to stab myself in the face with a broken beer bottle or to stab her ... she let loose this little gem:

"By the way, thanks for not being ugly."

I disregarded the compliment and honed in on what was so shallow, so immature, and I just couldn't stand by idly any longer.

"Excuse me?" I asked.
"I said, thanks for not being ugly."

I imagine my mouth fell open here. But of course, she missed my incredulity and continued on with her monolog (she was good at monolog).

"See, no offense, but talking to guys in bars is so boring. And tonight, nothing but these hideously ugly guys have been talking to me and buying me drinks. But at least you're not ugly."

At least?

She continues: "To be honest, I can't stand ugly people. Like, it seriously hurts my soul to look at ugly people. Like, I honestly feel physical pain if I have to look at an ugly person."

I couldn't hold back anymore, "You must not own any mirrors then."

Her face: disbelief, horror, then anger — in that order, half a second max — then her fruity drink came flying onto my face, followed by a dainty slap.

"Asshole!"

She stormed back to her friends.

When I first started going out and trying to meet girls, I used to be horrified at the thought of something like the above stories happening to me. The idea of getting slapped, or a drink thrown on me, or getting thrown out of a bar, these were all nightmares that would probably have visibly shaken me at the thought of them happening. Maybe you feel the same way right now.

But both of these memories are still bright in my mind, as they're some of the most important learning experiences I had with women — even more important than many of my successes.

Believe it or not, being slapped by these women taught me a lot about attraction, as much as anything else that I've experienced. For starters, being slapped by a woman is not the end of the world, or even of the interaction. It's simply an emotional response. And as a highly emotional response, I'll always take being slapped over indifference or boredom any day. It's polarizing. And polarizing women is more important than being pleasant to them.

Being slapped also taught me that you can't always control how people react to you. Some people are completely out of their minds or they behave very inappropriately. You can't help this. You cannot control what happens in every interaction. The sooner you accept this, the better off you will be.

Sometimes you'll deserve being rejected. Sometimes you won't. I don't regret what I said to the sorority girl, though in hindsight, I probably didn't need to be rude to her — if that happened today, I'd just excuse myself and walk away.

As with any type of failure, it's not until you've been rejected a certain amount that you realize how insignificant it actually is, how you spent so much time worrying about nothing, and how you're free to act however you choose.

The reason men fear rejection is because they're operating on other peoples' truths, not their own. In fact, men who fear rejection tend to be oblivious to their own truth because if they were aware of their own desires, needs and values, what would they have to be afraid of? Why would they ever hesitate to expose their vulnerability to others?

Most men with weak grasps of their own truth fantasize about the ability to never be rejected, ever. Not only is this a manifestation of their neediness, but it's unrealistic. Being rejected saves me so much time and effort. If I had to go on a date with every single girl I found even mildly attractive, I'd probably lose my mind.

It's Usually Not About You

As soon as you realize that 95% of this attracting women stuff has nothing to do with you, is the moment you become free to pursue what you want without hesitation or fear.

When you get out there and start meeting a lot of women, you'll begin to notice that there's a lot to be said about "the right person at the wrong time." I can't tell you how many times I've met an amazing woman, but some circumstance was standing in the way. It happens all the time. It may be that she's on vacation and flying 2,000 miles home tomorrow. Or that she just got back together with her long-term boyfriend and doesn't want to screw it up. Or that her dog just died and she really doesn't feel like talking tonight. Or that her ex-boyfriend has been calling her and harassing her she just wants to be left alone. Or that the last guy who she went on a date with grabbed her ass and treated her like shit and he had the same name as you.

There are a million extraneous circumstances completely outside of your control and at any given time, a large chunk of the women you meet and talk to are going to be experiencing one of them. The best you can do is to let it go and remember: *it's not about you.*

This is why we pursue women based on *our* truth. This is why we polarize women as soon as possible. This is why we approach women looking to see if *she fits our values* and needs and not the other way around.

Most men, when they meet women, are thinking something like, "I hope she likes me," or "I hope she doesn't embarrass me or reject me." It's all about them. And therefore, when things don't go anywhere, the men take it personally — they get upset or angry or butt-hurt that this random stranger with breasts isn't laughing at their lame joke right now.

Instead of thinking, "I wonder if she'll like me," think, "I wonder what she's like?"

Instead of thinking, "I hope she doesn't reject me," think, "I hope I'll find out if she's right for me."

The beauty is that whether she falls in love with you on the spot or she throws a drink in your face… you've succeeded. You've found out the truth. Your curiosity is fulfilled and you can now decide whether you should move on or not.

I see every rejection simply as some form of incompatibility. Whether she thinks I'm a total creep, or she's crazy about me but we live on different continents, or she's in a horrible mood when I ask her out, or she thinks I'm cute but has different values and interests than me — whatever the reason, if a woman ever rejects me, it's because she's not compatible with me. It may be a permanent incompatibility. It may be a temporary incompatibility. But the point is that if she liked me enough, she'd be willing to work at making it happen with me. And if she doesn't, then that just means it's wrong person — or right person, wrong time. And that's fine.

Remember, it's "Fuck Yes!" or no. And if I'm not getting a "Fuck Yes!" then I'd much rather have a no than a "Meh, OK."

Redefining Success

The concept of "success" in modern dating advice is often skewed. It's influenced on the one side from traditional roles and rules — get a nice girlfriend, get married, etc. — and on the other side by unrealistic expectations and social pressures by other men — to be "the man," you have to bed dozens of women, that you should never be rejected, you should be banging models and "10's," etc. Men put a lot of pressure on one another and shame one another for being rejected and this develops an unhealthy culture of masculinity based around neediness rather than genuine self-expression.

Choosing how we define success with women is vitally important. If you choose the wrong way to define success for yourself, then the months or years of effort you put into achieving that goal will go to waste.

For instance, men who define success for themselves as how many women they can have sex with will waste away time pursuing and manipulating women whom they don't necessarily enjoy or aren't even that attracted to in the name of achieving the "success" which they've defined for themselves.

This isn't a shooting range we're on here. We're talking about the health of our emotional lives. Women and our relationships are one and the same with our emotional health, and so the way in which we perceive women and relationships is going to be reflected in our emotional well-being.

If you choose to believe "success" with women is determined by which woman chooses you or how much money you can provide — well, then there's a good chance you're going to be quite lonely followed by ending up with the nearest woman capable of tolerating you for a lifetime.

If you choose to believe "success" with women is a lay count or some other statistical data point, then your love life will become just as objectified as the women you meet, and although you'll have the quantity of interactions to back you up on paper, all emotional quality will be lost, along with your happiness.

I define success in a qualitative way: maximizing happiness with whichever woman/women I prefer to be with.

Success = Maximizing happiness with whichever woman/women we prefer

This may seem like an obvious statement, but the implications are actually quite profound. For most of the men in the world, their "success" with women is defined by:

Being married or not being single.

- Never being rejected.
- Dating a woman who is more attractive than his friends' girlfriends.
- How many women they can approach or have a date with.
- Quantity of women rather than quality of women.
- If she fits some stereotype of what "beauty" is.
- If she's the kind of woman you've been raised to think you should date.

When we define success as finding the relationship(s) that will maximize our happiness, our approach takes a completely new light. Instead of waiting and hoping for a woman to select us, instead of racking up numbers, instead of winning bragging rights, instead of avoiding rejections — our success is defined by screening through as many women as possible until we find the ones we enjoy and the ones who enjoy us.

Suddenly, rejection goes from hurting our success rate to often helping it. Having a great date with a woman who wants to wait to have sex with you can become a far greater success than that woman who bangs your brains out an hour after meeting you.

We screen through these women by polarizing them. We are polarizing them by sharing our truth with them openly and freely. And when we do this, women will either become incredibly attracted to us or they will reject us. Either way, we'll be the happier for it.

And not only do we pursue and polarize the women we believe will make us happy, but we also push the interaction. Some men become satisfied with how many women they can kiss or how many phone numbers they can collect. This is not success. This is not success because you are not *maximizing* your relationships with these women. These metrics are part of the process. There is no happiness inherent in owning more phone numbers than anyone else. You're chasing validation, not fulfillment. You are not dating them, sleeping with them, becoming intimate with them or even committing to them. Get out there and expose yourself. Open yourself up and find what makes you happy. Yes, that will mean you'll probably get hurt. But so what? The best things in life don't come easily.

So it's time to get into the nitty-gritty. So far we've spent most of the book being introspective and talking about our emotional lives. Whether we get any specific woman or not depends on our level of investment relative to our investment in ourselves. This is non-neediness. We build non-neediness through vulnerability. We practice vulnerability by being honest.

There are three ways in which we are honest. And those three ways will make up the bulk of this book. The three ways are 1) living based on our values (lifestyle); 2) becoming comfortable with our intentions (boldness); and 3) by expressing our sexuality freely (communication).

The first way of expressing our truth involves developing a lifestyle that makes us happy. The second way of expressing truth is by being courageous and fighting through our fears and anxieties. And the third way of expressing truth is by communicating well and being uninhibited in our sexuality.

Choosing to not live a lifestyle based on our values and interests is only being dishonest with ourselves. It reflects a higher investment in others than in oneself. Therefore, it is unattractive.

Not acting on our desires and asserting ourselves where appropriate is showing more investment in others than ourselves. It is therefore unattractive.

And not communicating our thoughts, feelings, and desires freely and clearly also demonstrates more investment in others than in ourselves. This is also unattractive.

Lifestyle, Courage, and Communication: I refer to these as the Three Fundamentals.

Chapter 6
The Three Fundamentals

The Three Fundamentals are the three ways in which a man can become more vulnerable and become less needy. Improving each one of the Three Fundamentals will improve your results, sometimes drastically. Each of the Three Fundamentals can be worked on independently, but as we'll see later, improving one of the three often indirectly benefits the other two and vice-versa.

The Three Fundamentals are:

1. Creating an attractive and enriching lifestyle.
2. Overcoming your fears and anxiety around socializing, intimacy and sexuality.
3. Mastering the expression of your emotions and communicating fluidly.

The way to improve each of these fundamentals is by drilling deeper into your vulnerability for each one of them. So one way to think about it is that the fundamentals are the *categories* in which you can improve your results with women (and general well-being), and expressing your vulnerability and seeking truth is the *process* in which you improve in the categories.

For short, I refer to the Three Fundamentals as Honest Living, Honest Action, and Honest Communication.

For instance, Honest Living, or creating an attractive lifestyle involves really drilling down and understanding what you want as a man for your life and then working to make that a reality. If you're in a job you hate with hobbies you hate and friends you don't like, then no matter what you do or how much money you make, you're going to have a hard time meeting attractive women that you enjoy and who enjoy being with you. This is because the identity you have adopted does not accurately reflect your emotional needs and desires. You are not living your life honestly, which means you are not investing in yourself, which means you are needy and unattractive.

If your true passion is art and you push paper around at an insurance firm, then you're not living honestly. You've compromised your identity in some way to fit what others have dictated it should be; in this case, you've given up what actually makes you happy in order to fit the values or roles of other people in society (having a stable job, working in the corporate world, having a nice house/car, etc.). This displays a lack of vulnerability and neediness.

If those things aren't *actually* important to you, then you have a responsibility to yourself to change. Otherwise, you're always going to be an unattractive man. How so? Because you're living 40 hours a week, every week, investing your identity in what others want out of you and not what you want of yourself. This is like baseline neediness, and until you straighten this out, you will be needy with *every* woman you meet, preventing you from meeting the truly amazing women that you could potentially be with one day.

Honest Living correlates directly with the *quality of women* that you will attract. The more in-tune you are to your lifestyle, the more you take care of your appearance and your health, the higher the quality of women you will attract and the greater percentage of Receptive women you'll meet.

Honest Action is overcoming your fear and anxiety around women. Our anxiety is another form in which we highly invest ourselves in others' perceptions and avoid our truth. Like a poor lifestyle, it also seems to be embedded in us and it's something that requires a lot of thought and effort to repair over a longer period of time.

I call it Honest Action because it is honesty in the strictest terms. If you see a beautiful woman and have a desire to meet her, to not take action and meet her is a form of being dishonest with yourself. If you're standing in a bar, and you see a woman who catches your interest, and you keep looking at her all night because you're afraid to do something, on a deep level, you're being dishonest about your intentions and sexuality. You're being overly invested in her and others' opinions and are unable to expose your vulnerability.

All fear around your sexuality is a result of feeling inferior or unworthy. If you're afraid to approach a woman, it's because somewhere inside you are more invested in her opinion of you than you are in your own opinion of yourself. If you're afraid to ask a woman to come home with you, it's because you are afraid of the sexual reality that you want to sleep with her

— you're more invested in her *not* rejecting you than you are in aligning yourself with your desires.

Overcoming your fear and anxiety will correlate with your overall results with women. The reason being that once a man overcomes his fear of rejection, he's willing to more or less pursue any woman he wants when he wants. Even if he's a deadbeat (lacks a good lifestyle) or even if he's terrible at expressing himself (lacks good communication skills), he will eventually meet women who want to date him and sleep with him by no other means than pure numbers. If he's willing to approach 500 women with no fear of rejection, eventually at least one of them is going to stick.

Honest Action correlates directly to the *quantity of women* you meet and attract.

The third fundamental is Honest Communication, or learning to express yourself freely and effectively. This is what most dating advice sells and classifies as "game" — a good sense of humor, the ability to connect with people, telling stories, engaging people's attention, having charisma, and expressing your sexuality openly. These are all parts of this fundamental.

I call it Honest Communication because it's learning how to communicate your true intentions and emotions to others clearly. Often we have certain thoughts or feelings, but we don't know the best way to convey those thoughts or feelings. This third fundamental focuses on how to do that.

Honest Communication will determine the *efficiency* with which you are able to attract women who are compatible to you. A man who communicates poorly or is unable to express himself clearly will lose a lot of romantic opportunities to "lost in translation" situations — misunderstandings, vague communications, inaccurate assumptions, etc.

Natural Advantages/Disadvantages

Chances are, you're already pretty strong in one or more of the Three Fundamentals and weak or mediocre at one or more of them. Where your strengths and weaknesses lie will determine not just the quantity of your results with women, but also the types of outcomes you achieve.

For instance, a man with an amazing lifestyle but poor action and poor communication will be surrounded by beautiful and interesting women but never be with them. Classic examples of this are rich or good-looking men who are still single and frustrated. They may have money, connections, power and meet beautiful women regularly (or have beautiful women approach them), but they're never able to capitalize on their opportunities.

A man with no fear or anxiety with women will be able to approach and ask out many women, but his effort-to-reward ratio will be poor and the quality of women will be worse. Often a lot of aspiring players fall into this category — they go out 5-6 nights per week, approach dozens of women, fail with almost all of them, but every once in a while convince a drunk sloppy girl to come home with them.

A man with great communication skills but a lot of fear and a poor lifestyle will rarely meet or attract beautiful women, but the few times he does, he will capitalize on his few opportunities. Most so-called "normal" guys are like this. They rarely see opportunities, but when they come along, they take them and do well. The problem with these men is that they never feel like they're in control of their love lives. They're always waiting for that next woman who's interested to come around. And sometimes they end up waiting quite a while.

The Three Fundamentals are interesting in that they explain why a lot of men implement a lot of dating advice or self-improvement and don't see any actual change in results. If your weakness is that you aren't able to communicate coherently or empathize with what other people are expressing, then being encouraged to approach 500 new women is going to be an absolute disaster.

If you are broke, live with your parents, and have no job, then being encouraged to spend all of your time and money out in nightclubs is only going to get you a bunch of meaningless sex with mediocre drunk girls who have no better options.

If you are scared to death of saying anything to a woman you find attractive, then the best conversation tricks, teasing and flirting lines, or even openers are not going to help you at all.

But as I said earlier, the Three Fundamentals are interdependent — they feed off of one another. So if your biggest problem is an inability to communicate well, then meeting 100 new women won't *directly* benefit you, but the fact that you're talking to 100 new people will indirectly help your issue. In the same way, being able to communicate effectively will help guys with extreme levels of anxiety in their development because the few times they do work up the nerve to make a move on women, they will usually do it in a smooth and socially-attuned way.

It's important to cater the advice that you implement to your specific issues. Hopefully reading this chapter, you have at least a vague idea of where your weaknesses are. The rest of this book is dedicated to breaking down each of the Fundamentals individually and giving clear how-to guides for improving them. Identifying and focusing on the fundamental(s) you need to work on most will be the quickest route to improving your love life and sex life. Most of you will have one or two main weaknesses and probably one natural strength. But some of you may be weak in all of them. I guarantee you, if you're reading this, you are not strong in all of them. If you think you are and are still reading this far, then you're deluding yourself and need to re-read Chapter 3 on being honest with yourself.

Two Types of Men

In my experience, almost all men who struggle with relationships fall into one of two categories: socially anxious or socially disconnected.

Socially anxious men tend to have the third fundamental down very well. They're good at expressing themselves and are very aware of social norms and what others are thinking/feeling. In fact, in a lot of cases, socially anxious men are *too* aware of what other people are thinking and feeling and, therefore, have a lot of social anxiety. They're afraid to speak to new women. They get nervous pushing things forward. They're scared to ask women on dates.

Generally, though, once these men *do* meet a woman who likes them, they do OK. They can converse with her all night. And if she happens to be attracted to him, he's not such a mess. But it's the actual being pro-active and making a move that scares him to death. These men usually spend most of their time focusing on overcoming fear and little time on expression.

Socially disconnected men are the opposite. These are men who have always been a little bit "oblivious" to what others think and feel around them. Usually, they're guys who have always kind of kept to themselves and grew up more interested in their studies or some nerdy subject than the people around them.

Interestingly, men who are socially disconnected have far less fear or anxiety when it comes to approaching, pursuing, or escalating with women. In fact, it's *because* they're so oblivious to social cues and what others are thinking/feeling that they are so fearless around them.

The struggle for men in this category is going to be the third fundamental: learning how to express themselves and understanding how people think and feel around them. These men have little hesitance or fear for action, but they tend to do the wrong actions at the wrong times over and over and over, and they rarely understand why.

The first fundamental (lifestyle) is all over the map and is a work-in-progress for everyone. The better your lifestyle, the easier everything else will be. And ultimately you should be working on your lifestyle for yourself first and foremost — the attractiveness to women is just an enjoyable side effect.

But the second and third fundamentals are intimately connected to one another. Anxious guys are anxious because they're so socially attuned to others (perhaps even *too* socially in tune with others), and socially disconnected guys are fearless because they are socially disconnected from others.

The idea is to become socially connected *and* fearless at the same time *and* have an awesome and attractive lifestyle. The full package. The Three Fundamentals.

But whichever type you are, read all three sections, as even reading about areas in which you're naturally strong will reinforce your positive habits. And you will probably pick up a few pointers on how to improve your strengths even further.

Part III is about Honest Living — building an attractive and abundant lifestyle so that quality women who are most compatible with you naturally gravitate into your life.

Part IV is about Honest Action — overcoming your fears and anxieties so that you may act on your impulses and desires without hesitation or shame.

Part V is about Honest Communication — training yourself to express yourself openly and effectively in a dynamic and interesting way that will keep women interested in you and help you make that transition to becoming physical with them.

Parts III and IV are divided into two chapters each. The first covers the concepts and ideas of that fundamental and the second gives specific, actionable advice on how to improve each fundamental. For instance, in Part III (Honest Living), Chapter 7 covers the concept of Demographics and how it affects how women are going to respond to you. Chapter 8 is called "Lifestyle and Presentation" and describes how we can use the knowledge of demographics to make ourselves as attractive as possible to each woman we meet.

Part V has four chapters to cover all aspects of communicating efficiently (verbally, physically, etc.), as well as what's socially expected in the courtship process.

And keep in mind moving forward that the foundation behind all of the advice given is the idea that an honest expression of yourself and your desires as a man is the most effective way to demonstrate non-neediness and to therefore create lasting and genuine attraction with women who will make you the happiest.

If at any point along the first six chapters you felt like something didn't make sense or didn't "click," then you may want to flip back and review it. If not, if everything makes sense and the reasoning behind everything I've said so far makes sense, then you're ready. Read on...

Part III: Honest Living

Chapter 7
Demographics

Before we get into what to say to women, how to make them laugh, where to take them, how to kiss them; before we even get into basic questions like what to wear, or how to look, what to say first, we have to ask a more important question. A question whose answer will affect and change everything listed above.

Which women do you want to meet and what kind of relationship do you want to have with them?

Context. Whether you chat a woman up in a coffee shop, introduce yourself at a business networking event, or attend a speed dating event is going to make a huge difference.

This question of where and in what context you meet women is what I call *demographics*, and it is by-and-large ignored by pretty much all dating advice out there today. This absolutely boggles my mind since social interactions are always contextual, and therefore, attracting women is always contextual.

Some dating advice tells a 40-year-old divorced banker meeting women at an art gallery the same advice that they tell a 19-year-old college kid sneaking into house parties. This is stupid. These two men have completely different priorities, life experiences, personalities, and interests, and the women they're going to meet in those two locations are going to be different in age, education, values, emotional development, appearance, and interests. That some advice would give these men the exact same lines or strategies to use just goes to show how completely out of tune a lot of men's dating advice is today.

The theory of demographics is simple and easy to remember: like attracts like. You attract what you are.

If you're a successful professional who likes fine wine, studied abroad and dresses well, chances are the type of women you're going to naturally meet and attract in your everyday life are going to be similarly educated, similar looking women with similar interests and similar success.

When demographics don't match up, then it causes friction. And as we learned in Chapter 3, friction prevents attraction from turning into intimacy and/or sex.

A common demographic mismatch scenario that I've seen many times is the nerdy guy who decides to try and become a player. Let's say we have a 35-year-old engineer named John. John has been a bookworm and shut-in all his life. He's had two serious girlfriends, both lasting more than five years each. He's recently single and has decided that he wants to date and meet as many women as possible before he gets married. So John reads some pick up artist book and begins hitting the nightclubs with the new "techniques" he's learned.

Now, let's ignore the lines he uses for a moment — in fact, let's assume the lines he uses are good (even though they're probably not). He approaches a very hot blond girl named Jenna.

Jenna is 20-years-old and in her second year at community college. She comes from a worse part of town and has been working a retail job at a shoe store for the last few years to put herself through school. Jenna has no clue what she wants to do with her life. In fact, she has trouble thinking about the future. She's gone into debt buying clothes and spends more time at parties than studying or doing homework.

John has three degrees, has spent the last eight years working 60 hours per week and never drinks. He's maybe been to 20 parties in his entire life and has only been drunk twice. He's passive and analytical and his sense of humor is highly intellectual. He's soft-spoken and thoughtful. He's not dressed entirely well and his hair is unkempt. He wears big glasses and is slightly shorter than average.

It's not hard to see that when he meets Jenna, no matter what he says or what line he uses, it's going to end quickly, and chances are Jenna is not going to be subtle about her lack of interest in John.

John may come away blaming the lines he used for not working. Or he may blame himself for being ugly or being a little short. But the fact of the matter is that it's just a simple incompatibility. John's values don't line up with Jenna's. Jenna's lifestyle and interests don't mesh with John's. John is older but less experienced. Jenna is younger but more experienced. John is mature and practical. Jenna is immature and impulsive. There are mismatches going on all over the place.

But let's keep the thought experiment going. Let's say two years go by. In those two years, John works on himself. He dresses impeccably now — wearing high-quality clothing and designer brands that are not only stylish but reflect his successful business persona. He's well groomed. He's gone to the gym and buffed up, gotten contacts instead of glasses and paid a stylist to fix up his hair.

John's also discovered how to lighten up a little bit and enjoy a party now and then. Occasionally, he goes out with some of his new young professional friends to have drinks and a little fun. He's begun spending more time at the beach and has been teaching himself the guitar on and off. His social confidence has soared, and his lifestyle has expanded and grown.

Jenna has also changed in the past two years. Since she last met John, she's dedicated herself to her studies. She just got into nursing school and has been taking it seriously and realizes she's smarter than she thought she was and that, at times, she actually enjoys learning. She also got out of a one-year relationship with a football player who was irresponsible and treated her like crap. She's realized that she needs a man who is more responsible than she is and that she needs to stand up for herself and expect more out of the men she dates.

This time, when John approaches her (lines or not), they suddenly have an overlapping demographic: John is now an attractive, well-kept, successful bachelor who knows how to let loose, have fun and express his emotions; Jenna is now not only beautiful but also responsible, ambitious and confident.

And like that, there's now mutual attraction.

Now, it's true that if John practiced and perfected his use of lines and tactics, he may be able to convince Jenna in the short-term that he's less invested and is actually in her demographic (vague stories about his stripper ex-girlfriends and the like), but hopefully by now you realize how badly these kinds of strategies backfire, particularly in the long run. Eventually, John's lines will run out and like Cinderella after the ball, Jenna will be horrified at who she's actually talking to.

101

But because John (and Jenna) worked on themselves, broadened their demographics, enriched their lifestyles, and lived their lives in ways that were more in line with what they wanted, they came to find enough common ground to be attracted to one another.

This is the power of demographics.

And notice it has little to do with the people themselves — whether or not they're attracted to each other — but more to do with timing. Two years prior they were not compatible. Two years later, they are. Remember, right person, wrong time.

If she loves to ski and ride horses, and you hate the outdoors and traveling, then that's going to cause friction — perhaps not immediately, but at some point.

If she values expressing her emotions openly and what her friends think of her, and you value serious conversation, intellectual pursuits and don't care much for social gatherings, there's going to be a large amount of friction from the get-go.

This is unavoidable. Clever lines won't change it. Being good-looking won't change it. Being rich won't change it. If you hate what she loves and she hates what you love, it's not going to go anywhere. Period.

The answer isn't replacing your identity and passions; the answer is to expand your identity and passions. Expand it to include new and interesting activities, new modes of expression, and new ways of presenting yourself.

Demographics explain why you meet women you just "click" with sometimes, and why, more often than not, you meet these women in situations where you're having fun and doing what you love.

Lifestyle Choices

The theory of demographics has advantages as well: if you play to your strengths — i.e., if you focus your time and energy on meeting women in situations where they are likely to share your values, interests, and needs — then you're going to not only experience a much higher degree of success, but you're going to meet women you enjoy a lot more.

For instance, I love to travel. And I love meeting women who love to travel. It's absolutely my favorite thing to talk about and typically if I find a well-traveled woman, I find it very easy to attract her and date her.

When I'm in a random bar in Texas, I rarely meet women who have traveled. But when I go to a European wine tasting in New York, I almost meet nothing *but* women who love to travel.

Or even better, if I actually get up and go to another country and meet other people traveling in that country, I'm going to have an extremely high hit-rate with those women.

If you love dancing or different types of music, then chances are the women you're going to meet at various dance events and concerts are going to be more compatible with you and you're going to have much more success with them.

Bars and nightclubs are generally considered "meet markets" or the obvious places everyone goes to meet someone. But think about the people and context in which you're walking into in a bar or nightclub: a high-energy, generic party situation, where people value having fun and spending time with their friends.

Assuming you're a guy who loves to party, have fun, and hang out with a bunch of new friends, that's great. But if you're not that naturally outgoing social type, then chances are you're not going to be very compatible with most of the people there.

It isn't until you develop that aspect of your personality or lifestyle that those women will begin to open up to you.

What I recommend to every man before he even begins talking to women is to sit down for a while and ask himself a few questions:

- What do you value in a woman? Honesty? Beauty? Affection? Intelligence? Curiosity? Similar interests? Education? Obviously, the answer is "all of the above", right? So let me rephrase the question: what do you value the *most*? What is an absolute deal-breaker in the women you date? Prioritize what you look for in a woman. This will help you decide where to look.

103

- Women with the traits that you value, where do they frequent? Where are you most likely to find them?

- What do you enjoy doing most? Do you love to read/write? Do you play music? Do you enjoy sports and competitions? What are the events or organizations that you can become involved in that explore your hobbies?

- If you don't know what your passions and interests are, take a minute and write down things that you've always wanted to do but have never had the time or never worked up the nerve to do. Make a promise to yourself to get involved in that activity or event in some way.

Obviously, not every interest is going to be overflowing with women. If you are a competitive chess player, you probably won't meet many women at chess tournaments. But few people have only one passion or interest. And chances are that you have at least a few things that you're interested in that are overflowing with women.

Here are examples of some great hobbies/events that you can use to meet women:

- Dance classes (salsa, swing, ballroom, etc.)
- Political organizations or events
- Concerts and concert promotions
- Amateur sports leagues (ultimate frisbee and co-ed volleyball tend to have a lot of women — women in good shape too)
- Volunteering, charities, charities events (usually overloaded with great women)
- Training courses (leadership, public speaking)
- Cooking classes
- Yoga classes (a goldmine)
- Meditation courses and retreats
- Self-help seminars and educational events
- Travel groups (i.e., couch surfing)
- For the religious: a church or whatever your faith's equivalent is
- Educational classes (foreign language, CPA, etc.)
- Dog parks
- Wine or beer tastings
- Art galleries, exhibits or showings
- Business networking events

Also, meetup.com and livingsocial.com are excellent resources for finding like-minded people and cool events going on in your city.

I have a friend who is an excellent dancer and goes to the local dance events in the every week. He's successful, smart and professional. He's cultured and well-traveled. He also networks through European entrepreneurs living and working in the US. Between these two groups, he meets tons of people and tons of attractive, intelligent women. To kick things off, he often brings them together by hosting events at his house. His consistent success with women comes not just from his charisma and his "game," but the fact that he's narrowed down the demographic of women who he likes and who are apt to like him and acts on it.

A much simpler example is another friend I have who is a professional musician. You would think he'd be getting laid all the time, but he actually spent most of his time in the studio and rehearsal rooms. That's where the real payday was.

But when he became single again, he began taking cheap and easy gigs, playing weddings, dive bars, in cover bands, etc. and quickly met more women than he knew what to do with.

In my own life, I have a strong passion for traveling and culture. Wherever I go, I make a point to join local events or classes where I'll meet other like-minded people who also travel. When I'm in the US, I spend my time at venues or events that are likely to have foreigners.

Whenever I'm in the US and I meet a woman from say, Argentina, and I immediately start telling her about the three months I lived in Buenos Aires — in Spanish — it's pretty easy to get a date with her, as you can imagine.

The answer for you is going to be completely different. You'll have to experiment. These are just some successful examples.

Demographics affect every interaction you have with women. If there is too large of a demographic mismatch, then the friction will be incredibly high, and no matter how attractive you are, she will not be able to connect with you.

This may explain a fair amount of failure you've had up until this point.

Expand your interests and pursue them.

If you're interested in spirituality and meditation, pursue it. If you're interested in politics and being active in your community, pursue it. If you're interested in food from around the world, pursue it. Take up cooking classes, food tastings, restaurant openings, etc.

Beliefs and Self-Selection

Lifestyle choices play an obvious role in the demographic of women we would like to meet. If you like to do yoga, and if you go do yoga, you'll meet other women who like to do yoga. They'll likely be attracted to you and you'll likely be attracted to them. Duh.

What's not quite as obvious but just as important, if not more important, is how our beliefs naturally screen the women who come into our lives. When I say beliefs, I mean beliefs about women, sex, relationships, and ourselves.

The idea is that our beliefs are reflected in our behavior, and behavior determines which (and how many) women are attracted to us.

For instance, if you believe all women are sluts and untrustworthy, then the only women who are going to be willing to tolerate your judgmental attitude are promiscuous women who are untrustworthy. Social psychology refers to this as the *assortment effect* and it's been demonstrated in many studies.

Another example is the belief that women want and enjoy sex as much as men do. This belief was a big one for me. Many men don't believe that women actually enjoy or fantasize about sex.

So how would this belief affect your behavior and screen the women who are attracted to you?

If you believe women don't or shouldn't enjoy sex, then the women who do enjoy sex will most likely not feel comfortable expressing their sexuality around you. And the women who do not enjoy sex will feel like you understand them.

Thus, you'll be stuck dating a bunch of women disconnected from their sexuality and uncomfortable having sex with you.

But if you believe that women do enjoy sex, then the women who do enjoy sex will feel comfortable expressing their sexuality around you,

106

while the women who are not comfortable expressing their sexuality will not be comfortable around you. Yes, this will invite rejections, but remember, rejections are a form of screening for demographics and in this case, it's doing you a favor.

You'll end up with a bunch of sexual and sensual women who enjoy being with you. Nothing wrong with that!

The assortment effect through personal beliefs is incredibly powerful. I think that most "problems" men try to overcome with tactics and techniques could easily be solved by simply questioning our beliefs.

I always like to tell men, "The only thing all of the women you date have in common is you." What I mean by that is if all of the women you date end up lying and being manipulative, or if all of the women you date are selfish and treat you poorly, or if all of the women you date are meek and have no personality, then likely there is something in your beliefs and behavior that is naturally screening for those types of women.

A blunter way of putting it is: whether you realize it or not, the results you get with women are always your fault.

Unfortunately, questioning and re-evaluating our beliefs about women and relationships is far harder and more uncomfortable than simply memorizing a pick up line or two. That's why most men don't ever bother doing it. And that's why these men never experience long-term success.

I think acknowledging your beliefs and also being able to acknowledge that they may not be true comes back to what was discussed in Chapter 3: being able to take an open and honest look at yourself and your desires. Becoming a non-needy man requires, first and foremost, a high level of honesty with yourself. Part of that honesty with yourself involves observing and challenging your own beliefs. If you have lived your entire life believing women are untrustworthy or that women who express their sexuality are immoral, then perhaps you should evaluate what kind of women those beliefs are going to attract into your life. And if you don't want to attract those kinds of women, perhaps you should experiment with changing your beliefs.

Now you're probably saying: "Experiment with changing my beliefs? How the hell do I do that?"

You change your beliefs by simply accepting the fact that you don't know what you're talking about and then you open yourself to coming to other conclusions. If you believe that all women are evil and manipulative, consciously decide that you may not know what you're talking about, and then go out and test new hypotheses out in the real world. Go to an event and pretend that all of the women you meet are loving, caring, and honest. Get online and message women imagining that every one of them is interested in you for you and not for some ulterior motive. See what happens. Sure, it will freak you out at first, but you'll quickly notice a shift in the caliber of women you attract and your relationships will improve.

Because here's the amazing thing about people, both men and women: people tend to conform to what we expect of them.

For instance, let's say you get a new job and your new boss immediately assumes you're a dick. He talks down to you, rolls his eyes at you, and acts as if your mere presence is an insult to everything he stands for.

How would you end up behaving towards him? That's right, you'd start acting like a dick. He treats you badly because he expects you to be a dick. And you start acting like a dick because he's treating you badly.

The same is true with women and dating. If you meet and date women believing fucked up stuff about them, you will only encourage that fucked up behavior. If you never trust the woman you're with and are always jealous, then you're just going to encourage her to do things behind your back. After all, she's going to get yelled at by you anyway, so she decides to start withholding information.

If you're condescending and treat a woman like she's a child who can't make any decisions for herself, then she will act like a spoiled child and stop making any decisions for herself.

In the therapeutic world, this is often referred to as "enabling:" when our shitty behavior encourages the people around us to adopt shitty behavior.

Demographics, and more importantly, analyzing our beliefs about relationships before we even start pursuing one, allows us to avoid these problems before they even happen, to avoid the disastrous breakups before they can ever occur.

Because ultimately, we attract who we are. And if we are a mean, vindictive, jealous or distrustful person – well, who do you think you'll end up being with?

Age, Money, and Looks

The touchiest part of demographics — and possibly the touchiest subject of *all* dating advice — is that of age, money, and looks.

I want to get this out of the way and make it 100% clear. Age, money, and looks matter — in some cases a lot, in other cases, not a lot, but they still matter. And anyone who tells you that they don't matter is lying.

With that said, age, money, and looks don't matter nearly as much as most men think. And if you're aware of the effects of demographics, you can work around them and even work them to your advantage.

When it comes to age, studies show that men's physical attractiveness peaks at around 31 (a luxury considering women peak around 21) and that our physical attractiveness recedes far slower than it does for women. In fact, studies have found that the average 45-year-old male is still considered as physically attractive as the average 18-year-old male.

The main reason is that studies have also found that women judge a man's status far less on actual physical dimensions and far more on style, grooming, and how men present themselves. As men, we're extremely lucky in this regard. Taking a man from a baggy beer T-shirt and ill-fitted jeans to a nice suit with a professional haircut will immediately bump him up 50% in the looks department overnight, whereas with women, it's a constant and never-ending battle to maximize their physical appearance as much as possible.

How to be as good-looking as possible will be covered in depth in the following chapter, but for now, just know that no matter how ugly you think you are (and chances are, you aren't), there's hope for you. And we'll take care of it soon enough.

Money is nice in that it demonstrates success and implies other positive attractive traits. But again, its utility is vastly overblown. When it comes to money, once again the surveys and studies have some interesting findings.

The first is that money/success matters more depending on your age. The older you are, the more money you're expected to have and the more successful you're expected to be in order to be attractive. The other finding is that the less wealthy *she* is, the more important money will be to her.

This is why the stereotypical gold-digger is usually a very beautiful young woman who grew up in poverty. Women who grow up with money or have money usually don't care about it as much.

But the fact remains that women perceive men with money the same way we perceive women with good looks: as social status. How each woman defines social status and whether money is a part of that or not is going to vary from woman to woman.

Which brings me to my primary point when it comes to age, money, and looks. Again, it's about the demographics.

I saw a quote recently that said, "Only lazy women are interested in men with money, because they don't have anything else going for them."

Ask yourself for which demographic of women are looks and money highly important? Women who tend to *only value* good looks tend to be women who *only have* good looks and little else to offer. Women who are highly interested in money are going to be women who don't have other interests or opportunities in front of them.

What I'm saying is, women who *only* care about things such as looks and money are usually going to be women who you're not going to be interested in or who are not going to make you happy. So you're not missing out on much.

With that said, everybody values looks and success to a certain extent. So it's not something we can write off completely. You *should* be as good-looking as you can possibly be. And you *should* be as financially successful as you can possibly be. And even the most interesting and well-rounded and psychologically healthy women are still going to prefer a good-looking and successful man to one who isn't. All things equal, looks and money always increase your odds.

But I would just add the caveat that you should be as good-looking as possible *for you*. You should be as financially successful as possible *for you*. These are just other avenues in which to invest in yourself.

So yes, looks and money matter. But the question is, how do they affect our results with the majority of women?

The more money/looks/success you have, the less attractive behavior you need. The less money/looks/success you have, the more attractive behavior you need.

Another way to think of this is that age, money, and looks are universal demographics, and therefore, an incompatibility in any one of them is apt to cause extra friction everywhere.

But just because there's friction, or just because there are fewer Receptive women, it's no excuse for not having success in the long run.

The vast majority of men who get hung up on looks and money get hung up on them because they're using it as an excuse. It's absolutely not a valid excuse. A guy who is good-looking or rich still has to work for his results; he just doesn't have to work as hard as the next guy.

Trust me, I've coached hundreds of men who were far more professionally successful than me and far better looking than me, yet I still dated more women and more beautiful women than them. Being good-looking and being rich is worth nothing if you don't *do* something with it. You can be the richest guy in the world, but if you behave like a timid, negative and weak chump, then women will still be repelled.

And as we'll discuss in the next chapter, anyone can be handsome and appear high-status if they put enough effort into it. So no excuses.

And of course, status is ultimately determined by demographics. At a college house party, a burly 20-year-old kid who crushes beer cans on his head is going to have a high level of status to the girls there. At an opening at a local art gallery, he is going to have almost none. A skinny bass-playing hipster is going to have high status at a local indie show and low status at a business-networking event. A successful stock trader who wears Armani suits is going to have high status at his firm's annual Christmas party and little status at a hippy music festival.

It's all relative. The key is to 1) recognize your personal interests and strengths, and 2) build upon those personal interests and strengths to quickly attract women in your preferred demographic.

Social Proof

The concept of social proof comes from influence psychology and is well documented in everything from salesmanship to advertising, to politics, and to attraction and relationships.

The idea is that as humans when we see many other people valuing something, we will unconsciously value it ourselves. For instance, if everybody else is talking about a new movie, we are more likely to want to see it because we'll unconsciously assume that it's a good or important movie to see.

This works with people as well. If you're at a party and someone walks in and everybody in the party stops what they're doing to turn and say hello to that person, your first thought would probably be, "Wow, who is that guy?" Chances are you'd want to meet him as well.

The idea is that this applies to women and attraction as well. If *you* are that man who walks into a room and everybody stops what they are doing to talk to you, then the women in the room are more likely to perceive you as high status and be attracted to you. Or if you're a man with whom multiple women are flirting, then it's going to incite even *more* women to begin flirting with you.

This is one reason why men in power — celebrities, athletes, etc. — are desired by so many women. The goal, as a man, is to cultivate as much social proof *within your demographic* as possible.

So, for instance, if you are a high-powered executive at your firm, then you have a large degree of social status and social proof at work. Chances are, the women who work with you are going to have some degree of attraction for you. But if you go to a bar on the weekend and know nobody there, then your social status is back to nothing. You're just another man there.

Social proof only functions within a demographic itself. That's why once you've narrowed down your demographic, you want to cultivate your connections and put yourself into as big of a leadership position as possible. Don't just join the intramural ultimate Frisbee team, start organizing it. Don't just volunteer at a charity event, help find sponsors for it. Don't just go hang out at a local club, but become a promoter for it.

Part of living the honest lifestyle is to pursue what you're passionate about to the fullest extent. If you absolutely love visiting art exhibitions, don't just visit a bunch of art exhibitions, but take an active role in the organization, start a meet up group to find other people who want to visit them, or create a forum for commentary. Don't just pursue your interests, become a leader in your interests. Don't just choose a demographic of women to meet, dominate the demographic.

Hopefully by now you're getting a clearer idea of what demographic of women you're currently attracting and which demographic of women you'd like to attract. In the next chapter, we will get into specifics on how to pursue the correct demographic for you and become as attractive as you possibly can be.

Being Something Versus Saying Something

If there's one takeaway from this chapter, it's that it is far more powerful to *be something* attractive rather than to *say something* attractive. You can say the most attractive sentence in the world, but if it isn't backed up by who you are, then it's not going to have any meaning. Whereas if you *are* something amazing, then anything you say will be attractive because it will be coming from a genuinely attractive man.

Women are attracted to your identity. Words mean nothing. What you say is only a means to buy you enough time to show her that identity. Notice I said "show her" not "tell her."

For instance, imagine you meet two different men. One of them is a scrubby, ugly, and shady character. He can't look you in the eye. He smells bad. He mumbles to himself and scratches himself in inappropriate places. While you're talking to him, he looks at you and says, "You know, I get a good feeling from you, you're someone worth knowing."

How would that make you feel?

You'd probably get the creeps and want to get away from him as quickly as you could.

Now imagine you're talking to a handsome, successful man who is charismatic and charming. Everything he says is fascinating and interesting. Then he looks you in the eye and says, "You know, I get a good feeling from you, you're someone worth knowing."

How would that make you feel?

It'd make your day. Why? Because the second man *is* someone. He's not just saying interesting and charming things, but he *is* interesting and charming. Suddenly the words that come out of his mouth have a whole new weight and meaning.

Again, a lot of men take this as another invitation to perform. Last night, I was in a restaurant with my girlfriend. It was a nice and expensive restaurant. A couple sat down at the table next to us. They were clearly on a date. The man was a bit older and the woman was young and beautiful. The man immediately closed the menu and said, "Don't order anything, I know something special that's not on the menu and you're going to eat it." The woman kind of meekly said, "OK." The man then argued with the waiter about cooking some mystery dish that wasn't on the menu. The man and the waiter went back and forth and soon it was apparent to all of those sitting in our section that something awkward and unnecessary was taking place. The woman became bored, irritated and was soon deeply enmeshed in her phone, checking Facebook, Instagram, Twitter, anything to get her away from this bonehead sitting across from her.

In the man's mind, he probably saw himself as a successful, powerful man. What I saw was a pathetic performance, overcompensation, a keen narcissism. A successful man doesn't need to prove he's successful by ordering something not on the menu. A powerful man doesn't have to decree to his date what she's going to eat that night.

This is why trying to impress women by flaunting an image of what you *think* is attractive will always backfire. Men can go out and perform as much as they want — for weeks, months, or even years — and they'll never get good results because they're not portraying themselves well. They don't have a clear and successful identity. They aren't in touch with the way in which they're living their lives.

When you're like this man – when you're focused so much on performing rather than actually being – then you are out of touch with your identity, who you are, and what you want. And when you're out of touch with yourself, you will fall into the abyss of vague and empty demographics. You will aimlessly claw for whatever woman comes near you. You will be left bewildered at how you seem unable to polarize anyone.

Discovering your truth and establishing your identity is necessary to determine the demographics of women you desire and the demographics of women you appeal to. And, as we'll see, working your demographics underlies everything else in dating.

Hopefully this chapter has helped you question what you're doing with your life, what your identity is, what you want out of your relationships, and what kind of women you'd like to attract.

The next chapter is going to get into specifics on how to build up an attractive lifestyle within your chosen identity and within your chosen demographic.

Chapter 8
Lifestyle and Presentation

As men, we're prone to assume that women perceive attraction in the same way we do. Science and psychology show that this isn't the case.

Men judge female beauty by physical traits first, personality and presentation second: high cheekbones, facial symmetry, waist-to-hip ratio, breast size, etc. As such, we often fall into the mistake that women judge our attractiveness with the same metrics; hence, obsessions with bench presses, height, and penis pills.

Yes, physical measurements play a role in how a man's appearance is judged, but research shows that other factors are more important.

That's why I draw the distinction between being good-looking and being attractive. Not everybody is born good-looking. But any man, with some time and effort, can become attractive. And in the end, what women want is a man who is attractive.

For some reason, many men believe that their physical appearance is set in stone and they rarely have any interest in altering it or making any major changes. What they don't understand is that the same man can present himself in varying ways, some of which are far more attractive than others.

Here are a couple unfortunate truths. The first is that appearance is extremely important. The difference between being perceived as stylish and unstylish is night and day. Yes, you can still be dressed like a bum and get girls, but the difference in the effort-to-reward ratio is massive. A makeover and wardrobe change can make meeting and dating women three times easier literally overnight. Not to mention all of the psychological side benefits of making you feel more confident, more interesting, more excited, etc.

Remember, your outward appearance is a reflection of your self-investment (or lack thereof). And your level of self-investment will make you less needy towards others, therefore making your behavior more attractive. If you don't put a lot of time and effort into how you look and how you present yourself to the world, women look at that and make unconscious assumptions about your status as a man.

The first and obvious step involves grooming and general maintenance. That means regular showering, shaving and haircuts, wearing deodorant, brushing and flossing your teeth, keeping clean fingernails, and wearing clean clothes.

I should not have to be telling you this stuff, but just in case I do, there it is. The above paragraph is non-negotiable, starting today.

There, now let's move on to the two biggest factors on your appearance, the two F's: Fashion and Fitness.

If these two F's don't excite you or if your immediate thought is, "Oh, I'll skip this and go straight to the pick up lines," then I hate to break it to you, but things aren't going to get any easier. People are always talking about what the "magic pill" to attraction is. If there was such a thing it would be the two F's. Bar none, fitness and fashion will do more to attract women in a shorter amount of time than anything else you can do. Being in decent shape and dressing well will make *every* phase of the process easier and smoother, from meeting women, to attracting them, to getting physical with them, to dating them, to staying in a relationship with them. There literally is no downside to either one.

So listen up and make a serious commitment to yourself, because if you don't make a commitment to yourself then nobody else will.

Fashion and Fitness

Many straight guys are averse to exploring their style and how they dress because they think it's "gay" or intrudes on their masculinity. It makes most men feel uncomfortable. A lot of men feel set in their ways and don't like the idea of changing the type of shirts they wear, or the haircut they've sported for years and years. They're also intimidated at the idea of standing out or looking too different from the people they hang around.

If this describes you, then it is going to be a mental hurdle that you'll have to overcome. Recognize that unless you've spent a large amount of time focusing on fashion and style already, chances are what you think looks good right now is not accurate at all. You may think you dress well —

hell, *everyone* assumes they dress well before they know better — but really it's likely that you don't.

So the first step is recognizing what you don't know.

There are a few rules to dressing well:

1. Wear clothes that fit.
2. Wear clothes that match.
3. Dress to your personality

We'll go through and break each one down, one by one:

<u>Clothes that fit:</u> To start, the vast majority of men don't wear clothes that fit them properly. Men often prefer comfort and practicality to any aesthetic purpose of wearing clothing, so most of their clothing is too big. Chances are most of your clothing right now is too big. Many men are also self-conscious about their body, so they buy large clothing to mask it.

When it comes to clothing, fit is king. You can have the nicest, most expensive clothes in the world, but if they don't fit well you'll look like a clown. On the other hand, you can have some modest or even mediocre clothing, but if it fits well (and you're in decent shape), you'll look quite good.

Fit makes a massive difference and the change is immediately apparent:

The first step to overhauling your wardrobe should be to go through your closet and pull out anything and everything that does not fit well.

You should always know your measurements. If you're not quite sure, ask to get measured. Most clothing department stores have a tailor who will gladly take your measurements for you.

With shirts, the shoulder seam should extend to the end of the shoulder, not any further. If it extends past the end of your shoulder, then the shirt is too big.

On dress shirts, the cuffs should not extend past the wrist bone.

The bottom of your pants or jeans should rest gently on the top of your shoes (unless you have a specific style of rocker or hip hop jeans). There should not be more than one "break" in your jeans — a break is a natural fold from them resting on the top of your shoe.

If you're stepping on the back of your pants with the heel of your shoe, they're too long. If your jeans are raising up to expose your socks when you walk, they're too short.

Your pants should never sag from your waist when you wear them, even when leaning or bending over. Plumber's cracks are never attractive.

Jeans should also never slip off your waist without a belt. Most men wear jeans that are too large for them and feel awkward when they first put on a proper-fitting pair of jeans. They feel tight and uncomfortable at first. But this is normal. You'll get used to them in time.

Here's an example of jeans that don't fit:

And an example of jeans and T-shirt that fit well:

A blazer that's too big; notice the shoulder seams sagging off the sides:

And another outfit that fits very well:

<u>Matching:</u> Men have an unbelievable knack for being oblivious to colors and how to coordinate them.

Matching is actually simple once you know what to look for:

- Your belt should match your shoes and/or your accessories.
- If you're wearing dress pants, your socks should match your pants.
- If you're wearing jeans, your socks should match your shoes.
- Your accessories must all be gold or all silver.

Here's an easy way to get started. Go out and buy a "black set" and a "brown set." Buy a nice pair of black shoes, a nice black belt, and a black jacket. Then buy a nice pair of brown shoes, a brown belt, and a brown jacket.

Then buy a few pairs of nice designer jeans with lighter and darker washes and a dozen or so shirts.

Then, it's just mix-and-match.

You pick a pair of jeans, a nice shirt, and then throw on your "brown set" or your "black set"— whichever set compliments the shirt and jeans the best. I like to wear the brown set with lighter shirts and jeans, and the black set with darker shirts and jeans.

Of course, dressing gets more complicated than this, but this is an easy and fail-safe way to start out.

Dress to your personality: Many men learn about fashion and then decide to buy some ridiculous stuff that does not suit their lifestyle at all: a 40-year-old business executive with baggy jeans and a hoodie, a 20-year-old college student with a $500 suit and sweater vest, or just all kinds of random stuff — LED light belts, gold clock necklaces, top hats, etc. It's amazing sometimes what people think is being stylish when it's really being outlandish.

You are not stylish if you are not dressing to your personality.

There are various fashion-based stereotypes considered attractive by women that you can model your own style after: the skater/surfer look, the successful businessman look, the rock star look, the athletic look, etc.

For instance, if dressing like a rock musician fits your personality, then do it. If you're a top accounting executive, you should dress like a stylish and successful businessman. If you love hip-hop and DJ, then you should dress more along those lines.

Look through magazines and get on the internet. Find famous people or role models who represent your personality. Then model yourself after those people's appearance.

Finally, if you're struggling to get a jump-start on fashion, you can get a fashionable female friend to take you shopping.

Good female friends are good assets if you're clueless about shopping, sizes, and what looks good on you. They can educate you and give you an unbiased female opinion on what looks hot on you and what doesn't.

But be warned, just because they have a vagina doesn't make them a *de facto* expert. Many women aren't as knowledgeable about fashion as they seem. Also, many women will try to dress you to their idea of a hot guy, not necessarily what works best for you.

Fitness: I'm not going to get into the nitty-gritty of fitness in this book because there are so many resources out there already. But I'll make a few basic points.

> 1. Exercise, no matter what. This is not negotiable. Beyond simply making you look better naked, exercise boosts your energy, raises testosterone, relieves symptoms of depression and anxiety, and generally makes you feel better about yourself.

> The exact way that you exercise isn't as important as the fact that you do it. If you like to play soccer, then find people to play soccer with. If you like to do calisthenics and yoga, then pursue that. If you want to hit the weight room and get big, go for that.

> 2. Clean up your diet. An easy starting point that will give you 80% of the results for 20% of the effort is simply cutting out the following things: sodas, fast food, desserts, and candy. If you just cut those things out of your diet, you'll see a drastic improvement.

> There's a lot of info out there on low-carb, high-carb, high-protein, low-fat, and so on and so on. Nutrition information is a sea that you can easily drown yourself in.

> But if you start with the most fundamental basics and cut the above things out of your diet (and start exercising regularly), it's impossible to not see major benefits within a few months.

And again, similar to exercise, nutrition goes beyond making you look sexy. It makes you feel better, gives you higher energy, makes your sex better, increases your moods, and can even save you a lot of money.

Body Language

Body language is something that can also be fixed in a relatively short amount of time and can immediately make you appear more attractive.

Some studies claim that body language accounts for as much of 60% of all communication that occurs between two people. That's a lot.

Considering all of the discussion we've had about neediness, intention, and sub-communication in the beginning of the book, the importance of body language shouldn't surprise you.

Major body language problems can be addressed consciously and with practice. But your body language will continue to improve as a side effect of becoming less needy and getting plenty of exercise.

To analyze your posture in this section, you will need the help of a mirror (preferably full-body).

1. Start by facing the mirror and then turn 90 degrees to the right or left. You should have a perfect "side view" of yourself. Now look at the "ridge" that extends from your neck to the end of your shoulder. If you're wearing a shirt, look at the seam that extends from your neck to your sleeve. That seam or ridge on almost everyone will be slanted forward. Move your shoulders back until that ridge or seam is straight — going straight from your neck to your shoulder. That's the optimal position for your shoulders. Remember that position and remind yourself to hold your shoulders there as often as possible.

2. Next, turn and look directly into the mirror, with your shoulders back, raise your chin up until it's at a 90-degree angle with your neck. Your eyes should be looking dead-ahead now, straight into themselves in the mirror, or aiming straight at the horizon as if you were walking. Make the back of your neck as straight as possible with your back. Notice when you pull your head up like this with your shoulders back, your stomach naturally comes in, and your back naturally straightens up. This is what we want!

3. Next, look at your feet. They should be shoulder-width apart. Take note of which way your feet are pointing. They should be pointed straight ahead or slightly outward at the most. If they're pointed inward or very far outward, this will cause posture problems and make you walk funny. Turn them straight ahead or at a slight outward angle and hold them there. If they continue to point in or out (especially when you sit down), it means that your calf muscles are too tight, and you need to stretch them or roll them with a foam roller.

4. Now, it's time to walk. Hold the position you're in — shoulders back, head up, back straight, stomach in, feet straight — and then slowly step in front of you. As you walk, you want to swing your shoulders. Not too far, because that'll make you look ridiculous, but move your shoulders as you walk. This will create swagger and make you look more relaxed as you walk. It will probably feel weird looking straight up and ahead while you're walking, but this is good. You want to be able to look everybody in the eye as you walk by them.

5. Finally, swing your arms slightly. If you don't swing them, you look robotic. If you have them in your pockets, you're either cold or a pussy. If you swing them too far, you look ridiculous. Just give them a slight swing… to go along with your swagger. There.

Practice this a few times until you can remember how it feels. Take note of the feeling and then force yourself to go back to this position as much as possible.

Go step-by-step if you must. As you walk down the street, remember: shoulders back, chin up, eyes straight, feet straight, shoulders swagger, arms swing. Always look straight ahead. Don't ever look down at the ground unless you think you're about to trip. Look people in the eye as they walk by — particularly attractive girls. You'll catch people making eye contact with you. You'll feel the urge to look away. Don't. Always make other people break eye contact with you before you break it with them.

Do it until it becomes a habit.

Challenge yourself to go out for a week straight and do this every time you're in public. Notice any changes in how you feel. Notice any shifts in people's reactions to you. Notice any shifts in your confidence.

Vocal Tonality

Vocal tonality is definitely overlooked by men. It's not just having a sexy voice that's important; it's having an expressive and a *loud* voice.

We actually have two "voices": a "head" voice and a "chest" voice. Basically, when you sing, your head voice does the high notes and the chest voice does the low ones. Your head voice breathes out largely through your nose while your chest voice through your mouth. The head voice comes from the throat and the chest voice from the diaphragm.

Try this exercise. Hum a note, then slowly raise it and then slowly lower it. It should sound like a siren, up high, down low, up high, down low. As you do this, pay attention to where the air pressure in your body is. As you shift from high to low, it goes from your head to your chest, and then back up again.

As you could guess, we want to develop that chest voice. Again, the only way to do this is through conscious practice — reminding yourself countless times to speak from your chest voice until it becomes a habit.

Here's a cool exercise that you can do. Read the following sentence aloud:

"Do you want to get a drink Thursday night?"

Now, hold your nose and read it again. How different is your tonality? If it's not very different, you already speak largely from your chest and probably have good tonality. If you suddenly sound very nasal when you hold your nose and say it, you need to work on speaking with a deeper voice.

Keep practicing it until you can say it while holding your nose and it doesn't sound any different.

Another problem men have is they often talk too quickly. This comes from a subconscious belief that if we don't get everything out quickly, people won't listen to everything we have to say. This is a needy behavior.

There's not a definitive metric for this. But pay attention to whether people seem to have trouble hearing you often. Experiment with slowing down how you speak and notice any differences in how it feels or reactions you get. If people are constantly asking you to repeat yourself, and it's not loud in the room, you may speak too quickly.

Also, chances are you are not loud enough. In fact, just about everyone does not speak loud enough. Speak louder. Do it now, do it everywhere. Don't scream. But speak loudly, from the diaphragm, from your chest voice. Research shows it commands more respect and attention.

Like body language, these adjustments will take time and practice to implement.

Not only do better body language and vocal projection engage other people more effectively, but good body language has also been shown to affect your moods positively. Yes, even shifting your body into a more confident position consciously will make you feel more confident and vice-versa. Even if you do it on purpose and know what you're doing, it will still work. So start paying attention to your body, how you present yourself, how you sit, how you stand, and the amount of eye contact you're making. It makes a difference. And it adds up quickly.

Developing Character

One thing that consistently holds men back is that they come across as just another typical dude or bro. Dime a dozen. We're pressured most of our lives to go with the flow, go along with what our friends like and just agree with what those around us think.

As we've discussed, this is unattractive behavior because it demonstrates a lack of investment in your own interests, passions, and desires. Attractive men are polarizing and uninhibited. Attractive men make their opinions known. They've had unique experiences and ideas. They've tried things many people haven't tried, done things many people haven't done, and share their ideas openly and freely.

Put another way, an attractive man with depth and character is a man who has opinions and openly expresses those opinions.

When it comes to deciding what one likes and doesn't like, most men have very lukewarm reactions one way or the other.

"Yeah, that movie's awesome," or "Yeah, I like that one," or "No, I don't like that show." It rarely goes beyond that. There's no sharing of *why* one prefers one type of music over another, one movie over another, one author over another. And there's no connection to the *emotions* driving that preference.

For instance, a random Joe may say, "I really liked *Terminator*. It was pretty cool."

A more interesting person may say, "*Terminator* was great. But what's more interesting to me is that it was the first movie I can remember in which you ended up rooting for the villain."

There's nothing wrong with being amiable and enjoying similar things to your friends. But one thing that will always make you stand out, particularly to women, is if you've not only expanded your horizons, but you've also made your own decisions about your personal tastes, your experiences, and what you think about various topics.

Let's be real, out of 10 men the typical single woman meets, 9 of them are into the following things: sports, comedy movies, rock and/or hip-hop music, and other generic guy activities. Again, nothing wrong with this, but what's going to make you stick out?

We want to shape you into a man with taste, a man with opinions, and a man who can explain exactly why he likes or dislikes everything from 70s Motown records to German films to 19th-century literature to impressionistic art. Don't get me wrong, I'm not about to tell you to go take a bunch of art classes or whatever. You don't need to be a super-intellectual snob. This is about developing your own opinions and enriching your life.

Too many men let their opinions be dictated by pop culture and their group of guy friends.

"Oh dude, Will Farrell is soooo funny."
"The new Batman movie is awesome."

Few men ever stop and actually think critically about *why* they like certain things, *why* certain forms of pop culture are popular and others are not. Few have the curiosity to look into new art forms or hobbies and figure out how they feel about them.

Here are some concepts to keep in mind as you go through your life experiencing art and media:

1. Assume everything has a form of value; it's your job to find it. Nothing is stupider than to be prejudiced against a genre of music or type

of movie for no other reason than because of some stereotype or preconceived notion about it.

Drop all of this prejudice and adopt this mentality immediately: "there has to be *something* to this form of art, otherwise it wouldn't have a following, so I should find out what that something is." Once you find it, *then* decide if you like it or not. Whether you like something or not, you should always be able to appreciate it.

2. When expanding your horizons; start with what's generally considered the best.

Some forms of art will come easily and naturally to you. It takes me literally two seconds to identify rock music that is transcendentally good, or painfully bad. I've been listening to it all my life. Country? Classical? Bluegrass? That takes some more time.

Do the same with movies. Watch every movie in IMDB's list of top 20 movies of all time. Google critics' top 10 movies of all time lists and watch everything on there. Watch every movie that's ever won an Oscar for "Best Picture." That's a good start.

Now, you may be saying to yourself: "This is all nice, but reading Hemingway or developing opinions on Chaucer or Bach will never get me laid."

Well, touché. Although, I'll make the following points:

> 1. Being a well-rounded individual with opinions will expand your demographics by quite a bit. So yes, none of this is necessary if you want to date a woman who has no interesting opinions herself. But if you want to date brilliant, vivacious women with artistic sensibility, passion and class, then a lot of this is a prerequisite.

> 2. The second point I'll make is what my high school literature teacher always told us: "You read literature because you can never meet enough people." What I take from this is yes, even though reading Hemingway or Milton Friedman's economic theories may not directly get you laid, what it will do is develop your perspective to be more varied, allow you to be able to relate to more people's experiences and ideas, and generally have a wider body of knowledge for dealing with people in general.

Believe it or not, Hayek's economic arguments for libertarianism have influenced my perspectives on dating and relationships for the better. I know that may sound crazy, but it's true.

Anyone who has read a lot can tell you that the best ideas you take from a certain book often have nothing to do with the book you read.

Many men have been caged into the same day-to-day grind, wasting away, spending their life doing things they don't truly enjoy and that don't truly express their identity and personality.

- They go to work (often at a good job).
- They come home and unwind.
- They watch the typical sports/sitcoms/movies.
- On Fridays/Saturdays, they hang out with the same 3-4 friends.

Often I meet men who don't even have this much variability and balance in their lives. They're stuck in 60-to-80-hour-per-week jobs, or they work two jobs, they have absolute no hobbies outside their filling bank account.

Now, there's nothing "wrong" with the above list. It represents about 90% of the male population between the ages of 20 and 40 in the western world.

But again, that's the point: how are you going to differentiate yourself from the other 90% of men out there?

Ask yourself this: If you were lined up next to 10 random, single men from your town, what would make you stand out from them? Imagine a woman met all 10 of you in a row. What is there about you that would stop her dead in her tracks and make her say, "Wow, this man is unique?" What do you have that they don't? What can you offer that most other men can't?

Do you secretly write poetry in your spare time and hide it in your closet? Have you been skydiving three times? Did you climb a glacier in the Alps once? Have you tried eating things like snakes, worms, spiders? What have you done that's cool and interesting and has shaped you as a person?

What are your rough edges that people can't find anywhere else? What have you done that will make you stand out in her mind?

Bringing It All Together

Developing an attractive lifestyle is a long-term process. It requires a consistent and penetrating look at your actions, your habits and what you've chosen to do with most of your time.

Your job, your hobbies, your friends, your interests, are these things mostly a result of what was told to you or pushed on you, or are they things that you consciously evaluated and chose based on how enriching and passionate they made you feel?

These are important questions. No one can live your life but you. And as long as you sleepwalk through life not ever questioning or evaluating the lifestyle you've built for yourself, the same behavioral patterns are likely to creep up over and over again.

Men often don't totally believe me, but poor lifestyle choices afflict all of your interactions and communication when it comes to women. Poor lifestyle choices reflect a lack of investment in yourself, which in turn causes you to be less confident around others for validation.

I first noticed this when I worked with men who still lived at home with their parents. A lot of these men were great guys. They were smart, funny, caring, had interesting hobbies. Some even had a good job, but they stayed with their parents for other reasons (health, etc.)

Yet they got absolutely no results. Women never responded warmly to them, and they never seemed quite as motivated or as confident.

There's a certain baseline level of independence and self-sufficiency that your lifestyle must give you for you to be able to move forward. If you're constantly stressed by work, upset by your friends, and in poor health, then no amount of work on your anxieties and communication is going to help much. You're effectively putting a ceiling on your development and your potential with women. The other two parts of this book will not be much use to you. You can try, but I can tell you, you probably won't see much change in your results.

Get your life taken care of. Get healthy. Find a happy group of friends. Find a few hobbies that you love. Develop opinions. Start caring about what you spend your time doing. This increases your self-investment and will make you less needy around others. This, in turn, will give you the courage to take the correct action and the wherewithal to communicate effectively. This is honest living.

And once you're living a life true to yourself, your values and your ideals, then it's time to take action.

Part IV:
Honest Action

Chapter 9
What Are Your Stories?

I park my car in front of the gym and immediately pop my headphones into my ears. As I get out and walk across the parking lot, I catch a glimpse of a slender figure walking toward the door from another angle. I look over. She's hot.

We catch eyes and hold. She looks away, but only after holding my gaze for a half-second longer than most people would. An instant of sexual tension pops up between us.

She walks into the gym about ten paces ahead of me. I check out her ass. It says "PINK." It's those fuzzy kind of tight sweat suits girls wear sometimes. My mind immediately judges this. For some reason, I think she's trashy. I have to stop myself. What do I know? Nothing.

For a moment, we're at the sign-in desk next to one another. I start scanning in my mind for something to say to her. But before I can settle on something her phone rings and she answers it. "Oh god, one of those girls," I instinctively say to myself. Again I have to stop myself. I don't know her. But obviously, if I'm dedicating such mental energy to her, I probably should.

For a few seconds in my head, I toy with some logistical scenarios that would allow me to talk to her later — like pretend I have to go to the bathroom so I can come back and hopefully catch her off her phone. No, that's too contrived. I could just approach her in the gym while we're working out. But to be honest, that has never gone well for me in the past and I'm here to work out, not to make friends. Or maybe I do my workout and try to time it so that I'm leaving when she is. Then I would feel like a stalker. Theoretically, these things could work, but my mind's losing interest. My headphones are blaring and my mind is working its way towards the squat rack.

I'm not going to lie and say that despite all of my hedging and indifference that I magically came up with some miraculous line that saved the day. Because I didn't talk to her. In fact, I don't remember seeing her again or thinking of her until I wrote this. So I didn't save the day. But then again there was nothing wrong with my day and there still isn't.

I'm also not going to sit here, as is typical with these types of books, and chastise myself for bitching out, for being a pussy, and for not manning up. It's not *that* big of a deal. And I'm also not going to give you, my humble reader, yet another lecture on how you should never bitch out, how you should always, always, always talk to her, no matter what, you fucking pussy — even if she's at the gym, on the phone, juggling knives, doing a handstand, changing a flat tire or administering CPR — you *always* fucking chat her up, goddamnit.

Let's be honest, we all pass up dozens of situations like the above on a weekly basis, no matter how experienced or inexperienced we are. We've all let hundreds, if not thousands of opportunities go, usually without a thought or even realizing it. We've all done it. And we'll all continue to do it.

So I'm not here to rail on you to stop passing up opportunities. You already know the opportunities you pass up. And I'm sure by now you've had more than your fill of woulda-coulda-shoulda moments.

I'm more interested in the stories you tell yourself. The stories that we all tell ourselves.

When I got into this stuff years ago, I struggled with anxiety around women as much as anyone as I've ever met. I've coached hundreds of men since then, and I've maybe only met 3-5 guys who have had worse anxiety than I did when it comes to walking up to a random woman and speaking to her.

Jump to today. I rarely experience approach anxiety consciously anymore. That isn't to say I'm some sort of badass. I put in my time. I paid my dues. A lot of it was fun and a lot of it sucked and was humiliating. But I did it. I grew. And I'm a better person for it now. Through the basic rote exercise of meeting thousands of women in the most basic or ridiculous scenarios over the years, most of that palpable fear — the hand sweating, the fast breathing, the mind going blank — most of that is gone.

What's not gone, and as far as I can tell, what will never be gone, is a continuing internal resistance to change, whether it be through outright fear, or subtle subconscious thoughts trying to sabotage me. That never stops. I don't feel nervous anymore, but I do feel a dreadful judgment and boredom. "Only prissy girls wear crap like that," "Oh God, she's one of those girls who's always on her phone. I don't have time for this." Sometimes it happens pre-approach. Sometimes it happens 30 minutes in. Sometimes it happens on the second date. But always, these judgments aren't accurate portrayals of her. I don't even *know* her. Yet I'm judging her. It's a defense mechanism. My conscious fear has disappeared, but my subconscious resistance is still alive and kicking.

And from what I've observed, *everybody's* subconscious defense mechanisms are still kicking. The resistance doesn't go away. It just changes shape. Over the years, anxiety morphs into apathy, which morphs into arrogance. The resistance may come before meeting her or before kissing her or before having sex or before committing to a relationship. We all have our own weak spots, and those weaknesses each have their own form of resistance to the change we want. One boundary simply gets pushed back into another and another.

Whether you feel incredibly nervous before you approach, or if you procrastinate calling women you've met, or if you tell yourself that you suddenly magically "don't feel like" having sex when you're out on a date with a girl even though she's obviously into you and wants to go home with you, this is your subconscious resisting change. And your mind is inventing stories to explain that resistance. These stories have emotions tied to them, whether they're fear, boredom, anger, shame, or whatever — which contribute to keeping you in the same place you are right now. It's your emotional inertia. It's the status quo. The mechanisms wired into you to keep you there, safe. And we all have them.

Here are some other stories I've been telling myself lately: That I'm too good for these girls; it's my subconscious's favorite story right now. I tell myself, "I've been with dozens of women hotter/smarter/cooler than her, so why should I bother?" Yes, I recognize myriad things that are wrong with that thought. Yes, I realize I'm totally pompous and full of shit when I think that. But that's my point. We're all full of shit — a lot. All of our stories are. And we listen to them most of the time. We believe them. I know mine's dumb, just like yours probably is too. But that's what pops into my head. That's the excuse I have to fight through these days. And for me, this one is a constant battle.

Another one that's been surfacing a lot is that I don't follow up by phone/text enough because I feel like I've somehow earned the right to not put effort into my interactions with women anymore (if you ever wondered how teaching pick up and dating can kind of screw you up, there's a nice example).

I don't call girls back as often as I should. I feel entitled for some reason. Like they should feel grateful and just show up at my doorstep when I want them to. Sure, sometimes I genuinely don't really dig a girl and don't care if I see her again. But other times I do and I regret not putting in the extra effort a few weeks later.

These are my stories. They're completely different now than they were three years ago. And they were completely different three years ago than they were six years ago. But they've all had the same purpose: to protect the status quo. My emotional inertia.

What stories do you tell yourself? Because until you're aware of your stories, you're not going to be able to change your behavior. Maybe you get very nervous in bars and clubs and tell yourself stories of inadequacy. "Girls like that only like tall guys with muscles." Or maybe you tell yourself, "I'll start approaching after a few drinks." Or maybe you tell yourself that you're always in too much of a hurry, too busy to stop and say hello to a woman in a coffee shop.

Maybe you tell yourself that you need to have something really amazing to say for her to like you. So you stutter and stumble when talking to her, trying too hard and weirding her out. Here's a story to try out: maybe you're already amazing.

Or how about this one? Maybe you tell yourself that you're not even ready to meet women yet. You sit at home and read more books like this, telling yourself "Just a little bit more," or "After I get a raise and a new haircut," or "Once I save up to buy some nice clothes." And then once you get that raise, or get those clothes, then a new story pops up to take its place. You need to study more first. Or go on a diet. Then you'll be ready. Yet six months have gone by, and nothing.

It's always something, isn't it? There always seems to be something that you don't have right this second, that if you had it, you'd be able to act in the exact way that you'd like. Right?

So what are your stories? What do you tell yourself to justify that internal resistance inside you? And what stories can you tell yourself instead to remove as much of that resistance as possible?

People talk a lot about the idea of "skill" in all of this stuff. "Pick up is a skill. It needs to be practiced," blah, blah, blah. I think as the years go on, it's being proven over and over that what you say isn't so important, how you approach isn't so important. What's important is that you move things forward without hesitation, without that resistance that you're obeying right now by doing nothing, by remaining in the status quo — the same resistance I listened to today at the gym. That girl could have been the love of my life, the absolute perfect girl for me. Who knows? I never will.

The only important "skill" in dating is learning how to stop buying into your own bullshit, to stop believing your own stories. The resistance is constant. So you must constantly fight against it, acknowledge the stories you create for yourself, look them in the eye and say, "You know what, I don't care if she's on her phone and her ass says 'PINK' on it, I want to meet her." And then do it. Without hesitation. Without fear. And without apology.

Sure, you'll have to flex your mental and emotional muscles, and build up your body of self-awareness, but here's the good news: those are the muscles chicks actually dig.

Unfortunately, we all buy into our own bullshit. We all believe our own stories from time to time. And chances are, the more anxiety and fear you have surrounding women and your sexuality, the more of your own stories and bullshit you've bought into.

Defense Mechanisms

Most of us have a lot of fear and shame bundled up in our sexuality. These fears usually manifest themselves in a handful of very specific scenarios:

- Fear of approaching and starting a conversation with an attractive woman

- Fear of stating sexual interest either directly or indirectly (by asking for a phone number, calling a phone number, asking her out on a date, etc.)

- Fear of initiating sexual contact (typically the first kiss situation)

- Fear of actual sexual intercourse

141

The majority of men experience at least one of the above fears to some degree when it comes to interacting with women. There is a minority of men who will be completely devoid of one or more of the above fears and a very tiny minority who will be devoid of all of the fears above.

These anxieties are manifestations of neediness and an unwillingness to be vulnerable. Typically, the needier you are in a certain area, the more anxiety you'll have in that area.

This is unscientific, but in my experience coaching and working with hundreds of men, I've noticed correlations between high degrees of anxiety and experiencing one or more of the following situations: lack of a father figure growing up, emotionally abusive childhood, childhood traumas, strict religious upbringing, strict cultural upbringing, bullying or social ostracism growing up.

The sad fact about anxiety is that once you have it, it's there and figuring out why it's there doesn't help much. You can either avoid it the rest of your life, or you can do something about it.

We're here to do something about it. This section of the book is called Honest Action for a reason.

I personally think anxiety is the biggest culprit when it comes to preventing men from successfully meeting and dating women. You remove anxiety, and trial-and-error will take care of most of the rest.

Anxiety, almost by its very definition, represents a high level of neediness. Let's say a beautiful woman sits down next to you and you want to say something to her but are scared to death. The fact that you're scared to death demonstrates a high level of investment in her opinion of you, and thus a high degree of neediness. This neediness creates a fight-or-flight response in us — a surge of adrenaline, we begin sweating, our mind starts zipping at a million miles a minute, thinking of everything and nothing all at once — and if we do manage to utter a word, chances are we stutter and sputter and make a red-faced fool out of ourselves.

This then leads to further anxiety the next time a beautiful woman sits down next to us.

This is a terrible conundrum, and almost all of us suffer from it in some form or another. I suffered from it *horribly* and it took me years to undo it.

Hopefully, with what I learned, it won't take nearly as long or be nearly as painful for you as it was for me.

The first step to overcoming your fears is to figure out what your pattern is.

When we are confronted with our fears or anxieties, we have a pattern or strategy that we usually use to deal with them. For instance, my most common pattern is apathy. Whenever I'm confronted with something I'm afraid of, I pretend — or scratch that, *I convince myself* — that I don't actually care. Here are some of the most common patterns that I've noticed:

1. Blame Game — The Blame Game is where, when confronted with something he's afraid of, a man blames someone or something else for his fear.

For instance, let's say you're anxious about giving a presentation at work. Someone who does the Blame Game will come up with reasons why his boss is stupid and how he's way too smart to be doing this anyway and how it's not his fault if things go wrong because he's been sick and so-and-so didn't do enough research. In the context of women, the Blame Game will often result in men convincing themselves of stuff like, "Oh, she's stuck up," or "She's just into guys who are good-looking," or "She's too stupid for me anyway," or "This club is too loud to talk to people," or "Women in Miami are just bitches, I need to find a new city."

The excuses and blame can be petty and ridiculous, but they can also run deep. The awful part of the blame game is that with it come anger and frustration. And if you do it enough, the anger will pile up and you will end up with some pretty bitter and irrational beliefs about women. Men who have played the blame game their whole lives may develop screwed up beliefs like, "All women care about is how much money a guy has," or "All girls in bars are stupid and shallow." This can lead to some pretty dark places.

2. Apathy and Avoidance — This has always been my Achilles' heel, and it's quite common. Experiencing apathy and avoidance is exactly as it says: it's when a man convinces himself that he doesn't care or that it's not important to him. I did this for *years*. I convinced myself that I didn't care about meeting women and that it didn't really matter if girls I liked didn't find me attractive. Well, after enough

months of sitting home alone looking at porn while all of my friends were going through girlfriend after girlfriend, I had a rude awakening: I do care. Apathy and avoidance isn't the worst response when avoiding our fears with women in that it usually can't last forever. We're biologically compelled to pursue women so at some point, instinct will win over. Where it *is* dangerous is in other areas of our life such as career, family or hobbies. The apathy and avoidance pattern is the root behind the couch potatoes and disgruntled office workers of the world.

3. Intellectualizing — I guarantee that this is part of the reason you're here: you have some sort of fear, anxiety or pain related to women, and instead of actually *doing* something about it, you got online and decided to look up an answer that you could study.

Intellectualizing is sometimes beneficial in that you can learn a ton of information about a lot of subjects, and sometimes, the intellectualizing will lead to more self-awareness and help clarify what sort of action you need to take. But there are many men who use intellectualizing as just another form of avoidance. It tends to be really smart guys too, which is a problem, because the smarter you are, the more you're able to intellectualize and convince yourself that you need to learn and understand more.

But when it comes to women, this is not the answer (says the guy who wrote a 200-page book on women). Honestly, if you went out and talked to women for a year without ever reading a word of dating advice, you'd probably do OK, assuming you were honest with yourself and able to learn from your mistakes. Sure, this stuff all helps, but in the end, your best teacher is your experience. There comes a certain point where learning more about a subject is no longer beneficial and on the contrary, is just going to get you more mixed up and confused, since you have no experience to actually apply your knowledge to.

Intellectualizing also ends up having a backlash. Once you study a subject enough, it can actually increase your anxiety. By studying it so much, you've put more pressure on yourself to succeed and, therefore, build up higher expectations for yourself.

There are more patterns, but these three above are the main ones that I've run into with men trying to overcome their anxieties.

Also, there's a pattern within each of the responses to fear listed above: they aim to *avoid* the fear and they usually do it by *convincing themselves* of something that's not necessarily true.

The blame game guy will convince himself that it's her fault. The apathy guy will convince himself that it doesn't matter. The intellectualizing guy will convince himself that he needs to learn and understand more first. In the end, they're all avoiding what they're afraid of.

Also, realize that no one uses just one defense mechanism. We all use each of them some of the time. In fact, we may stack them on top of each other. For example, "I don't care what the girls think here because they're all stuck up bitches, so I'm going to go home," neatly stacks apathy on top of blame.

With that said, we all seem to have a favorite pattern that we fall back on the most often.

The key to overcoming your fears is first and foremost to break your patterned response to your fear. This requires a certain level of self-awareness and discipline.

So for instance, when I was learning to approach women, I had a lot of fear and anxiety. And my pattern was apathy. So I'd be hanging out in a bar, see a cute girl I liked, and my immediate reaction would be to say something like, "Eh, I don't really feel like talking right now," or "I don't feel like meeting girls right now." This was complete bullshit. I had purposely gone out that night for no other reason than to meet women. I had been reading books and websites all week about nothing but meeting girls. I wanted to meet girls.

It wasn't until I became aware of this pattern that I was able to start breaking it and forcing myself to talk to that woman I wanted to talk to, even when my mind was telling me that I didn't want to.

So here are some helpful ways to break your own pattern:

1. Take a moment and think about what you're most anxious about. Is it approaching? Is it showing sexual interest? Is it asking a woman out? Is it the first kiss?

2. Now write down your pattern with it. So for instance, "Calling women, pattern is apathy," or "Approaching women, pattern is blame game."

3. Now, create a goal for yourself, for instance, "Call every phone number I get, no matter how much I don't care." Write it down.

4. Tell a friend or a buddy what you plan on doing and ask him to keep you accountable.

That last item is important. Sharing your fears and having someone keep you accountable is integral to this whole process and makes it 10 times easier. Even the very act of sharing your fear with someone who can empathize and understand goes a long way towards relieving the pressure.

You Are Not a Victim

One assumption I've lived my life by for a long time now goes like this: "If it's a question of me being screwed up or masses of people being screwed up in the same way, then it's far more likely that it's just me being screwed up."

Just to name an obvious example. Men often come to me and say something like this: "I go out and try to meet women, but the problem is all of the girls in my town are catty and immature. So I guess I just need to move to a new city."

Really? So, it's not you who's screwed up, it's the 150,000+ single women in your city who are *all* screwed up — in the exact same way. What are the odds of that?

Or you get men who claim that *every* — not some, not most, but *all* — American women are fickle and too individualistic. Or that *all* women who dress provocatively are immoral cheaters and would never make a good girlfriend.

Men make negative assumptions and stereotypes about *millions* of women for no other reason than to shirk responsibility for their own shortcomings. This appears to me to be nothing but a victim mentality and it pervades a lot of men's thinking, some in more obvious ways than others.

This doesn't necessarily mean the general observations are wrong, it just means you're interpreting them in such a way to victimize yourself. Sure, American women may be more fickle and pretentious than their European counterparts (then again, they may not be). Women in your town might actually be more closed off than women in a bigger city (or they might not be). But you're choosing to let those observations be responsible for your own actions. This is the definition of being over-invested in others and being needy.

Humans stereotype for a reason: so that we can manage large chunks of information to orient ourselves more efficiently. Often, stereotypes can be useful. But usually they're not. Often they're nothing more than excuses — ways for us to avoid the blame and responsibility for not being satisfied with our results. And these excuses hurt us and shut us off from opportunities. If we're blaming others, we're not learning. And if we're not learning, we're not improving.

So returning to the "women in my town are cold" example. Yeah, they may, on average, be colder than say, Las Vegas women. But are *all* of them? No. Maybe 40%? 50%? But if you write them *all* off as being cold and use it as an excuse and not take responsibility, you're effectively shutting yourself off from 50% of the women in your town. You're effectively missing out on hundreds of opportunities.

The same goes for complaints against American women. There are something like 40 million single women in the US. And you truly believe you can't find one good one? Whose fault is that? It's your fault. You're being lazy. You're being lazy and unfairly judging millions of women all because you aren't willing to take responsibility for your failures.

I believe strongly in taking responsibility for everything that happens to you in your life. Our minds are always looking for ways to avoid pain and failure and rejection, and so they constantly churn out rationalizations to keep us impeccable; it's them who fucked up, not us. We're fine. We did everything right. It's that fucked up world's fault we're not happy.

Blame is yet another form of neediness. It's prioritizing others over yourself. As long as it's their fault, then you don't have to make yourself vulnerable.

But when you practice taking responsibility for everything that happens in your life, you stop blaming others. It becomes less a question of blame and more a question of sacrifice. It's no longer their fault that you're still

147

single because they're all cold bitches, but now it's your fault and a question of whether you're willing to sacrifice the extra effort or not to find a woman who isn't a cold bitch. Taking responsibility and morphing blame into sacrifice empowers you. It puts the ball in your court and returns you to the healthy reality that the only person in this world who determines your success and failure is you.

The question of blame, responsibility, and sacrifice is a profound one in relationships as well. Dysfunctional relationships almost always crumble under the pressure of one person blaming the other for their shortcomings or transgressions. Research has shown a direct correlation between the amount of blame leveled between partners and their propensity to break up. The recipe for a healthy and happy relationship is one where both partners take responsibility for their own emotions and their choice to commit to the other.

Earlier in the book, I mentioned that before I got into all of this dating advice stuff, I dated a girl for four years in high school and college. I was madly in love with her and she ended up cheating on me and leaving me for another guy. For a long time, I blamed her and I was very angry.

Rightly so.

But as time passed, I recognized a few things: 1) I wasn't exactly boyfriend-of-the-year, and in many ways, her cheating and leaving me wasn't very surprising; 2) there were plenty of warning signs that I chose to ignore or was just completely oblivious to; and 3) regardless of her actions, I made a conscious choice to commit to her day in and day out, and the risk of being cheated on was always a possibility in that commitment. The awful result of that relationship was a possibility I had been aware of from day one. Yes, she did something shitty, but I also chose to trust her.

In the end, I made the conscious decision that I was willing to sacrifice the risk of being hurt in order to enjoy the commitment of our relationship. And I wouldn't take that decision back. It was my responsibility.

When I was younger, I used to have a love/hate relationship for superficial party girls. I was young and had seen in a movie that I was supposed to be some studly party guy, and so I spent a lot of time trying to attract drunk party girls and have sex with them. It frustrated me for a long time and the 'hate' part of the love/hate was that I came to see them as fickle, stupid and shallow.

Now, that may be true, but I was blaming *them* for my lack of success with them. I mean, how dare they not be attracted to me! If they weren't so dumb, they'd be lining up to sleep with me, and that's how the world should be, right?

No, it shouldn't. That was an immature and entitled mindset to have. I was blaming them for something I was responsible for. And by doing so, I refused to respect them as human beings, and rather, I was choosing to see them merely as gyrating sexual pleasure objects that were to be conquered, like in a video game.

The truth was I had to make a choice: was I willing to work to expand my communication in order to connect with girls like that? At the end of the day, that's the only relevant question. The women you meet will be the women you meet, but are you willing to put in the effort to make something of it? When I did, I found something out: that many of them were not so stupid and shallow and superficial after all. In fact, many of them are smart, interesting and fun — and beautiful! But until I opened myself up to that possibility and took it upon myself to find them, I was missing out.

Challenge yourself to find the good and beautiful thing inside of everyone. It's there. It's your job to find it. Not their job to show you.

Sexual Motivation

Another problem a lot of men run into, aside from their fears and their anxieties, is a seeming lack of motivation to get out there and pursue women. It's one thing to sit at home and read books like this one, but it's something completely different to actually get off your ass on a Saturday and force yourself to meet women. It takes a lot of effort at first, and some men are easily able to convince themselves that it may not be worth the effort.

Since the advent of internet pornography, it's become easier than ever for men to satisfy their sexual urges. And today, there's an entire generation that has grown up always having access to as much pornography as they want since a young age.

There are a lot of anti-pornography movements, and there are even theories about "pornography addiction" that are thrown around. Although there's no absolute scientific proof (yet) for porn addiction, here's something I can tell you that is absolutely true: porn harms your motivation to pursue women in real life.

There's a bit of an epidemic of sexual apathy going on worldwide, where husbands, boyfriends and even single men are turning to pornography rather than the real life women that they see walking around every day. And it makes sense why: it's easier, the women are hot, the sex is more exciting, it's available at any time with the click of a mouse, it's (usually) free, the girls never say no, it's emotionless and there are no obligations or commitments involved.

The problem is that there are some negative side effects. The first being that porn creates very, *very* unrealistic expectations about sex, about women, and about sexuality. Porn makes money by accentuating and exaggerating sexual ideals. Actual sex with an actual woman often involves awkward moments of figuring out what she likes, what you like, who likes it which way. It also often involves ecstatic moments of emotional intimacy, something porn can never provide.

Also, real women, no matter how hot they are, have imperfections — imperfections that are covered up in porn by makeup and plastic surgery. If a guy gets too accustomed to the perfectionism of porn, he's going to have a lot more trouble becoming motivated by the girls he sees every day.

The other problem is that porn is so easy, that it encourages men to masturbate *a lot*. And as we all know, as men, the more we masturbate, the more interested we become in food and television, and the less we become in women and accomplishing something.

Napoleon Hill wrote a famous section in his classic work *Think and Grow Rich* called "Sexual Transfiguration." Hill noticed and theorized that extremely successful men also had extremely high sex drives. And not only did they have very high sex drives, but they also channeled this sexual energy into their work and their accomplishments. Often they would abstain from sex or masturbation for long periods of time and would, therefore, feel more energized.

Science is starting to back this up. Orgasms, or more accurately, ejaculation in men, actually causes a depletion of various hormones and endorphins which often lead to useful behaviors as well as motivation.

Men who have masturbated constantly since adolescence often masturbate so hard and furiously that they desensitize their penis to realistic scenarios. When you masturbate three times a day for years straight, you often have to grip yourself very hard and rub furiously to get off. This can often lead to sexual issues and impotence when a man actually does get into bed with a woman. This is because vaginas are soft, they're wet, and the sensations they give you are subtle. Your iron-fisted grip does a horrible job of preparing you for the warm lady love.

So here's what I recommend to you and all men who are looking to get motivated and improve themselves. It's my patented masturbation and porn diet that I give to men. In fact, I still go on this diet myself from time to time when I want to add a little motivation to my life. It works wonders, and a lot of men have gotten stunning results from it. I've talked to guys who literally sat around reading dating advice for years without ever taking action, but on my masturbation and porn diet, within two weeks they were out there meeting women and trying to get dates.

So without further ado...

- End all pornography immediately. Starting today. Delete everything from your computer. Throw out any discs or DVDs you have. And if you have trouble controlling your urges, download some free website blocking software and block every porn site you know of indefinitely. This may sound horrible or extreme, but trust me. You will thank me in a month.

- Limit your masturbation to once a week. Schedule it. Pick a day. I usually pick Monday. Do not deviate from your masturbation schedule! If you want even a larger dose of motivation (and you want to be as horny as a 14-year old), limit your masturbation to once every other week. Again, pick a day and hold yourself to it.

- When you masturbate, you're only allowed to fantasize about women you've met and have not had sex with. It could be that woman at work. That girl you met Saturday night. The girl you have a date with that week. Whatever. But she has to be real, and she has to be someone you have not slept with (but obviously want to).

- When you masturbate, use lotion or lube. Do it slower than usual. Drag it out longer than 10 minutes if you can. Take your time with it. Enjoy it. You don't get to do this every day, remember?

Follow this for a few weeks and you should find yourself motivated. If you mess up or give in, just start over again. Don't be hard on yourself. Ideally, within a couple weeks, the idea of going out to approach women should sound exciting to you instead of a chore. This is good. So go out and do it!

Chapter 10
How To Overcome Anxiety

Think back to the last time someone you didn't want to see tried to hang out with you. Maybe it was that annoying guy at work. Maybe it was your black-sheep brother-in-law. Maybe it was a blind date when your mother tried to set you up with her friend's daughter. Think of that awkward situation where you had to turn someone down. Think back to the last time you had to politely come up with excuses to not spend time with somebody. How did it make you feel?

Not good.

Rejecting people, whether you're doing it blatantly ("Go away and leave me alone") or indirectly ("Oh, I'm actually really busy this weekend, maybe another time") is actually an awkward and uncomfortable situation that nobody enjoys. Extremely few people in this world enjoy being an asshole or hurting someone else's feelings.

Now imagine having to do this on an almost weekly basis. There's nothing gratifying about it, in fact, it becomes frustrating and tedious. It also explains why women seem to complain about guys hitting on them or about guys being creepy — they have to reject them, and rejecting someone is generally an unpleasant or uncomfortable experience.

Men who have the perception of women as these ego-centric creatures who laugh at us from their sexual mountain-tops, doling out which man gets (a chance at) the divine pussy access and which man gets to squander away his time in solitude — it doesn't work like that.

Think about it. Why do women spend so much time and effort on their appearance? Why do they go to singles' bars and join dating sites and give blind dates a try? They don't do it so that they can revel in rejecting a bunch of guys. They're just as lonely and frustrated as we are. They want to meet a man. But not just any man, a great man — a man who is confident, charming, fun, and interesting. A man who is non-needy, who is vulnerable, and who will honestly express himself to her.

She wants you to be that man. She's secretly rooting for you. She doesn't want to reject you. Every time a new man walks up to her, she's secretly saying to herself, "Please, please, please be the man. Be the attractive man that I can't say no to." And then he nervously stutters around buying her a drink and makes uncomfortable jokes about the weather and she's back to that horribly uncomfortable position of having to reject him again.

Other times it doesn't even get that far. It's obvious before he even opens his mouth that it's game over. He's dressed like a clown or hasn't combed his hair in three months, or he's too drunk to even look at her directly.

This is also why women are willing to overlook a lot of bonehead moves and mistakes we make if they like us. It's amazing how many second and third chances a woman will give you if she likes you. She's rooting for you. She's your biggest fan. She's saying, "Oh, he chickened out on asking me out this time, but I'll find an excuse to call him so maybe he'll do it next time." They're begging for you to succeed. They want it just as bad as you do. That women at the party, in the coffee shop, on the dating site, they want you to be that unbelievably attractive man, that man who makes time stop for them and can make them feel things they've never felt before. They want you to be that. And when they reject you, it's not because they enjoy it, or because they have a big ego, or because you're too short or your muscles aren't big enough...

It's because you didn't give her that feeling. You didn't make her spin and fall and laugh and forget where she was or who she was with. That's what she goes out looking for: the man who can make her feel more alive.

The next time you make your move, when she sees you coming — and trust me, she usually sees you coming — know that she's already rooting for you. Secretly, she wants you to succeed as much as you do. And for a moment, she's your biggest fan.

And your role as a man is to take action. It's all on you. It's always on you. You move things forward.

And this is where the vast majority of men falter. An action as simple as opening your mouth, moving your feet in the right direction, or picking up the phone — they simply don't do it. The fear and rationalizations mentioned in the previous chapter are too large. It feels too overwhelming. And nothing gets done.

And ultimately, no matter how much you read, how much you study, how much you watch about dating and attracting women, if you're unable to take action, you will get nowhere.

Chances are if you're reading this, this is not the first book on dating or attraction that you've ever read. Some men become self-help and dating advice junkies, reading and reading and reading and never taking action.

In fact, sometimes men use reading and hoarding information and advice as a way to avoid taking action. They feel like if they're reading a 150-page book on attraction, then they're accomplishing *something* right? And as long as they're accomplishing something, then they don't have to confront what they're afraid of: going out and standing in front of a woman and expressing their truth, being vulnerable, subjecting themselves to rejection.

This isn't a new problem. The self-help and business advice industries have been dealing with it for decades. The men's dating advice industry has been dealing with it as well. But up until this point, it's done a piss-poor job of motivating men and helping to teach them how to take action.

The classic advice when it comes to taking action is more or less to jump into the deep end until you learn to swim.

The idea was that if you had a crippling fear of approaching women, then you sign up for a "boot camp" or program where a coach takes you out to a bar and more or less yells at you until you approach 25 women in one night. What you say and what happens is all over the place, but at least you're getting off your ass and doing something.

The problem with the overload method of taking action is that it's short-term and doesn't create a lasting habit. There's a simpler and less stressful method for achieving long-term results over your anxieties.

The Guide to Overcoming Your Anxiety

Fear is normal. Everyone has it in some form, and it's not going away anytime soon. The trick isn't to eliminate it; it's simply to train yourself to behave despite it.

Saying you want to get rid of all of your fear is like saying you want to get rid of all anger, or all sadness. This sounds like a noble goal, but research shows we instead suppress or avoid the emotions, leaving us less capable of dealing with them the next time they arise. Instead, what I recommend is to learn to adapt our negative emotions into positive behavior.

For instance, people with anger issues are encouraged to channel their anger through productive means — exercising, working, writing letters displaying their feelings, etc. To avoid or ignore the anger will only bring it back worse next time.

When my first girlfriend broke up with me, I made a conscious decision. I had laid in bed depressed for a week or two before I realized how ridiculous and pointless it was. I was hurt and I was angry, but laying around in bed and avoiding her was stressing me out. If I'm going to be stressed out, I may as well be productive.

So I decided to try another strategy. I decided that I would work on myself. I told myself I was doing it so that she would be sorry she ever broke up with me. I did it out of spite. My inspiration for self-improvement began with revenge.

For the first time in my life, I joined a gym. I began studying more. I went out with a female friend and bought some new clothes. I went to parties with new people I met. The whole time my motivation was the anger and hurt that I had towards my ex-girlfriend. I was going to become such an amazing person, she'd be sorry she ever left me.

The same concept can be applied to your fear and anxiety around women.

The other problem with interpreting the anxiety around women as something that must be removed is that this often only serves to amplify it. Neurobiology has shown us that attempting to avoid or shut out something we're afraid of only serves to make that fear stronger.

For instance, if you've ever played a sport and were in a situation where you had to hit one shot to win the game, you know that thinking about the pressure and the situation and *trying* to be relaxed about it only makes you more nervous and anxious.

The actual way to deal with it is to accept it, embrace it, and harness it to make your performance better.

In Buddhism, there's a saying, "What you resist will persist." And it's true in this case as well.

The proper way to handle your fear and your anxiety is to accept it, recognize that it's normal and a part of who you are, and to not even try to hide it from the woman you're meeting.

Think back to something you're very, very good at. Maybe you're really great at some part of your job at work. Or maybe you used to be awesome at tennis or chess back in school. Maybe you're a great public speaker.

All of those activities, when you were called on to put yourself on the line (major tennis match, big presentation, major meeting to lead), you probably got nervous beforehand. But did that nervousness make you crumble or did it invigorate you?

I used to love giving presentations in school. I was great at them. I used to get nervous before every single one. In fact, I've given probably 75 seminars and speaking engagements for my business over the past five years. I was nervous before every single one of those too.

But the nervousness almost felt good. I was confident in my ability. It was a borderline excitement. I knew I was going to blow everybody away. I knew that they would love me. So even though I was nervous to get up there, I couldn't wait.

It's like professional athletes who say they can't sleep the night before a big game. They're nervous, but they can't wait to get out there. They're confident in their ability and thrive on the pressure and the anxiety.

Psychological research actually shows that people perform better at activities under a certain amount of anxiety. In fact, what matters isn't the anxiety itself, but the person's confidence in their own ability to perform whatever action they're anxious about.

So it's less about the anxiety and more about how competent you feel you are. The less competent you feel, the more the anxiety will hinder you, the more confident you are in your ability, the more the anxiety will help you.

This is actually where a lot of dating advice and pick up theory actually hurts you. They explain these complicated models and theories, give you tons of material to memorize and practice, and present picking up women as some complicated task akin to rocket science that only works once you've tried and failed 1,000 times. That's going to scare the shit out of any guy with little to no experience.

The opposite is true. Attracting women is not complicated. And if you can have a conversation with a friend or family member, then you already possess the only "skill-set" required in attracting a woman. There's nothing to learn, only things to do. And the fear doesn't go away, you learn to hone it to help you.

I still get nervous every time I approach a beautiful woman I don't know. I've approached probably over 2,000 at this point. I still get nervous every time I go to kiss one. And I've probably kissed at least 300 at this point. I still get nervous every time I bring a new girl home. And I've slept with over 100 women.

The fear never goes away. What changes is my neediness and vulnerability. The difference between now and 2005 is that back then, I was incredibly needy and highly invested in how women perceived me. These combined to amplify my anxiety in ways that were unbearable.

See, a lot of people assume non-neediness means being fearless. But non-neediness simply means to feel the fear and not let it define you. Non-neediness is feeling the fear and deciding that something else is more important.

If I say or do something that screws everything up (and I still do all the time), I don't really care. It doesn't change how I feel about myself, and it doesn't change my confidence in my ability to interact with women in the future.

What's important is not the level of anxiety or fear, but your competence at whatever you're afraid of doing.

So now you're probably saying, "Well, that's nice, you're that confident because you've been with so many women, but what about a guy who has little to no experience with women?"

Glad you asked.

Like I said before, when it came to dealing with fear and rejection, all dating coaches basically took the approach of "throw him into the deep end and hope he learns to swim."

If you were afraid to approach random women, they would give you crazy lines or push you into very intimidating and difficult social situations, hoping to "scare you straight."

The idea was if they could put you in the worst possible situations, then the simple, regular social situations would stop being intimidating.

I guess it's like taking someone who wants to get in shape and putting them in a marathon right away. It'll help, but wow, it is *not* going to be pretty or pleasant. So that marathon — despite how ridiculously painful and difficult it is — will only give someone some good exercise once, not as a habit.

If that's it and they never exercise again, then they're going to revert back to their old, out-of-shape selves.

The same is true with our fears.

The way to attack anxieties is through incremental, consistent exposure. Not single, extreme exposure.

So for instance, you could take an afternoon or your lunch break each day and make a point to approach a few women just asking for the time.

Nothing more is required, just ask what time it is.

Find something easy, but repeat it regularly for a while, until it doesn't feel difficult anymore.

Then the next week, you go out and ask women what time it is followed by, "How is your day going?"

And each day, you slowly make it harder and more intensive.

Slowly work up until you're able to approach women by telling them you think they're attractive and asking them out on a date. You'll be surprised how quickly you can get comfortable doing this.

In fact, if you're like most guys and stick with it, then you'll begin to get hooked to the adrenaline rush and actually enjoy the butterflies you get when you approach a new woman.

Eventually, you'll be able to approach any woman in any circumstance and express your interest in her without fear, without worrying about what to say or what line to use.

And you can apply this to all sorts of situations: getting physical with women, emailing women online, calling phone numbers, sexual humor, conversations with women, etc., etc.

It's just a matter of knowing how to structure your exposure.

Afraid to kiss girls on a date? Challenge yourself first to hold their hand. Once you've done that a few times, then challenge yourself to put your arm around them and leave it there. Once you've done that a few times, then challenge yourself to kiss them on the cheek. And finally, challenge yourself to go for the kiss itself.

All of these goals can be done with the same girl, and even on the same date. But the important part is to stair-step your approach rather than expecting yourself to immediately be banging girls by the dozen after a week.

Get creative. Other sticking points this method can be applied to:

- Stalling out in conversation. Being comfortable talking about yourself.
- Calling girls and asking them out on dates.
- Going for sex once you've been out on a date with a girl.
- Flirting and teasing women.
- Showing direct interest. Stating that you're attracted to them.

Really all it takes is a focused and concerted effort on your part without actually expecting yourself to go from 0 to 100 in one night. Instead, you'll slowly but surely gain little successes repeatedly, not only building your competence and confidence but also making the whole process a lot more enjoyable, therefore helping you get over your anxiety.

And the great thing about this method is that as you get accustomed to your anxiety and become more confident in your ability, you'll be more motivated to meet and date even more women, increasing your confidence and competence further, and easing your anxiety that much more.

There's momentum to it, which is absolutely integral to developing a healthy and successful love life.

The last thing I'll say about this method before moving on is that you should only focus on one thing at a time. And when I say "focus" on one thing at a time, I really mean only quantify one aspect of your interactions at a time.

So if you want to be less nervous approaching women, don't bother yourself worrying about how to get phone numbers or when to go for the kiss or what texts you should be writing. Just focus on approaching.

But by the same token, when you're focusing on getting physical and assertive with women, don't worry about approaching. A very common form of avoidance for men who are terrified of "later stage" parts of dating women — escalating, dates, sex, etc. — is that they'll actually use approaching more women as a form of avoidance. They'll have a beautiful woman totally enrapt with them, and instead of seeing how far they can push things, they'll take her number and move on, because they tell themselves they want to keep "working on approaches." When approaching is not their problem. Getting sexual with women is!

Again, some self-awareness is critical. Take things one at a time, stair-step them slowly until you get not only comfortable with it, but excited about it, and then move on to the next thing. That excitement and enthusiasm will bleed over into the next form of anxiety and motivate you to keep going.

If this sounds like a lot of work, it's actually not. It's actually way less work. If you are afraid of meeting women, then it means just starting with the simplest step: ask for the time, join a dating site, ask a friend to introduce you. And then take it one step at a time, each step challenging yourself to do a bit more than before. It's actually quite simple and if you're focused about it and don't get distracted with all sorts of mundane and extraneous theory, it's very straightforward and can be accomplished quickly.

Courage and Boldness

Feeling fear and acting despite it builds courage. Anytime you're afraid to do something and feel some invisible force holding you back, yet you push through it anyway, you're building courage within yourself.

Courage is a habit. Courage is a form of discipline. It's taking a certain action even though you feel like doing something else. The difference here is that courage involves acting against fear, whereas discipline involves acting against laziness or fatigue.

161

Courage is built like a muscle. The stair-stepped exercises in the previous section are designed to progressively build your courage. The more courage you build, the more you'll be capable of bold actions. Bold actions require a lot of vulnerability and build non-neediness.

Stopping a woman and asking her for the time requires little courage and is not a bold action. It's well within social norms.

Walking up to a group of six people sitting down, asking to speak to the most attractive woman for a moment, telling her that you find her beautiful and you'd like to take her out sometime, is quite bold. It's bold because it requires a lot of courage to disrupt social norms and it requires quite a bit of vulnerability.

But there's a caveat here. You must *know* that you're interrupting social norms. You must acknowledge that what you are doing is unusual. If you don't, you'll be seen as someone who is out of touch and oblivious, which is not attractive.

This is a common mistake that many of the Social Disconnect types of men make. Since they're so out of tune with social norms, they often have no problem behaving in a bold way. The problem is, they aren't aware of when they're being bold or not.

For instance, I once worked with a guy who was very socially disconnected. We were in a shopping mall and we were walking around talking to women together.

As we were going down an escalator, we saw a very attractive girl going up the up escalator on the other side. As we passed her I mentioned to him that he should talk to her.

He immediately began running up the down escalator and shouting to her trying to introduce himself.

Obviously, this is a very awkward and strange thing to do. And had he been aware of how awkward and strange it was, he would have been bold. But instead, he was just unaware, and as such he immediately creeped the girl out.

This is why if you're ever going to do something that is unusual — approach a woman in a strange location, try to kiss her in a strange location, invite her out with you after just meeting her, etc. — it's important that you communicate that you realize what you're doing is abnormal.

"You know, I've never done this before, and I know we just met, but why don't you come to the restaurant with me?"

"Excuse me, this is kind of random, but I thought you were cute and wanted to meet you."

The bolder your action, the greater attraction you're going to create. The bolder the action, the more vulnerability you show, and the more you polarize responses.

If you walk around and ask women for the time, you are not polarizing them very much. Most of them will give you the time. The worst rejection you'll ever get may be, "Oh sorry, I don't have a watch," or something similar.

But if you walk around and ask women on dates, you're going to get polarized reactions — nervous and excited yes's, and tense and reserved no's. Or maybe a few angry no's. If you go even further and try to kiss a woman at an unexpected time, you're either going to get a very enthusiastic yes or an enthusiastic no.

The point is: greater boldness leads to greater polarization.

This is yet another argument for behaving in an assertive manner. This is also why one of my mantras that I tell men is, "Always err on the side of assertiveness."

Whenever you're in doubt of what you should do, err on the side of assertiveness. Choose the bolder action. Because if you wait around for the safer and less bold opportunity to make a move on her, chances are the attraction will be less or may even dwindle.

But bold behavior by itself will only go so far. Boldness must be molded by charismatic and efficient communication. Just behaving recklessly and will attract some women to you, and will give you sexual opportunities (particularly in party environments), but without communicating in a charming and interesting manner, and without being aware of social norms, it's unlikely you'll get many women to stick around, and your relationships will not be that enjoyable.

You can build up an incredibly attractive lifestyle and persona, focus on the proper demographic, act boldly and pursue women shamelessly, but if you can't communicate to them your intentions and your personality well, then it will be hard to maintain their interest for very long.

The fifth part will cover how to revamp your communication and how to make good impressions upon everyone you meet.

Part V: Honest Communication

Chapter 11
Your Intentions

All the way back in Chapter 3, we talked about how vulnerability only holds weight when it's communicated unconditionally — that is, when you compliment a woman or express yourself, you're not doing it with an ulterior motive, you're simply expressing yourself.

In this chapter, I'd like to take that idea further.

Men mostly communicate through facts, stories, and data. We discuss sports statistics, how we fixed our car last weekend, and where we plan on going next month. If a man says, "I'll see you at 6 PM," he typically means it literally. If a man tells you that he used to be the best basketball player at his college, you take it at face value, even if he may be exaggerating a little bit. If a man says he dislikes you, then it means he's not your friend anymore and you move on.

Women communicate more in feelings and, more specifically, through intentions. Sure, they still pay attention to the facts and stories on the surface, but what's actually communicated to them is the intention and feeling underneath.

This is sub-communication.

This is why your girlfriend can get upset and tell you she hates it when you spend time with your friends one night, and then the next night she insists you go to your weekly bowling league and not see any contradiction in her statements. On the first night, she felt like you weren't paying enough attention to her. On the second, she felt secure with you and wants you to be happy. The issue wasn't actually your friends, it was simply her feeling valued.

Needless to say, this sort of stuff often confuses the hell out of men, often for an entire lifetime.

This is why men often refer women to "crazy," "irrational" or "unstable."

The fact that men are oblivious to the emotions and intentions that underline everything women say often makes women feel like men are "heartless," "cold," "assholes," "selfish jerks," or that they "don't listen."

We listen, we're just usually playing in the shallow end of the pool.

In Chapter 3, I told the story of the time my friend walked around asking women if he could pee in their butt. Obviously, his words were absolutely ridiculous, and all of the women he approached — both the ones who rejected him and the one he went home with — didn't give his words much credit.

But his intention was loud and clear: I don't care what you think, I want to have fun tonight, and my idea of fun is a little extreme because I'm extreme. Obviously, this scared a few women off. But once he found one who liked his intentions, she latched on quickly and hard.

That's an extreme example, but here's another, much more common example.

Some dating advice tells men not to compliment a woman too early or too often. The reason for this is that most men who read dating advice have poor intentions: they're needy and looking to validate themselves through sex or female affection. So when a man compliments a woman out of neediness, it's going to make a woman feel uncomfortable and objectified.

Now if a man compliments a woman out of genuine appreciation for her, she's going to hear his intention and be genuinely appreciative of him as well.

Teasing and flirting with women is another great example. Many men, when they first begin trying to flirt with women, will tease them or "neg" them. Ask yourself this, what's the difference between a tease and an insult? Both are derogatory statements. Both often incorporate humor. So what's the difference?

Intention. Teasing is done with a fun and positive intention. Insults are done with a negative intention.

Or what's the difference between sharing yourself and bragging? Let's say you are friends with a celebrity. What's the difference between sharing your life experience with a woman (attractive) and bragging to her (unattractive)?

168

Hopefully, you're catching on by now: it's intention. What is your intention? Are you trying to impress her (needy) and therefore bragging? Or are you sharing yourself (vulnerability) and therefore polarizing her?

This relates directly back to what we talked about in Chapter 1 in regards to investment, neediness, and validation. A man who is extremely needy will have intentions dominated by seeking validation and approval and will therefore be unattractive regardless of just about anything he says. A man who is non-needy will have intentions dominated by vulnerability and will therefore be attractive regardless of what he says.

Obviously, there are technical considerations in how you communicate to people, which we'll cover throughout this chapter and the next. But the overarching point is that what you actually talk about has far less influence on your results than your intentions.

Everything in this chapter and next assumes you are acting based on the right intentions. Remember, women don't see your features, they see how you present yourself. They don't hear your words, they hear your intentions. If you suffer from chronic rejection, then you are presenting yourself poorly and/or have poor intentions. In both cases, you're needy, and therefore, you will always be seen as unattractive until you are able to invest in yourself.

Creepiness

The number one fear deterring men from openly expressing their sexual desires towards women is a fear of being perceived as "creepy."

Before we jump into what creepiness is exactly, and what women mean when they complain about it, I need to give the same type of painful-truth serum I gave for rejection:

There's no such thing as a man who is adored by women who isn't also creepy some of the time.

The fact of life is that if you are a man who expresses his sexuality freely (and you should), some women, some of the time, are going to find you creepy. It's simply unavoidable. No matter how cool, rich, good-looking and charming you are, at some point, somewhere a woman is going to be creeped out by you. Live with it.

So as a wise friend of mine sometimes says, "Give yourself permission to be creepy." Don't *try* to be creepy. And definitely don't walk around looking to intimidate women. Simply accept that sometimes, miscommunications happen, awkward situations occur, and things get misconstrued. Such is life. As long as you're respectful in how you express yourself, there should never be a serious problem.

There's no other way. And look, it's not the end of the world. There's no Creepy Police who come and handcuff you and throw you in Creep prison where you'll wait for you court date where you're charged for being creepy in the third degree.

Creepiness is one of these vague concepts that everyone knows, but no one can really put into words. If you ask women what creepiness is, they'll give you roundabout answers and inevitably fall into examples of creepiness rather than an actual definition.

Of course, their examples are all over the map and seem to have absolutely no rhyme or reason to them.

(For what it's worth, I asked a bunch of female friends this question and I got answers with examples of creepiness that spanned from "he had dainty hands" to "he grabbed me really hard on the arm for no reason," to "putting too many smileys in text messages," to "he looks at you in a funny way when he talks." As is often the case, women are terrible authorities on *why* they like/dislike something, all they know is that they like/dislike it.)

So, at the risk of sounding like a creep, allow me throw my hat in the ring and actually give a concrete definition for the phenomenon:

Creepiness is behaving in a way that makes a woman feel insecure sexually.

The further you get out of line with your intentions, the more distrustful she will be of your actions and words. And the more distrustful she is, the more insecure she will feel and the creepier you become. For instance, if you approach a woman and stand there and talk about the weather, but you're staring at her rack the whole time while licking your lips, then you will come across as creepy. Your actions and words are completely out of line with your intentions and she can see that.

Even if you tell her honestly, "You have great tits," you will be creepy. Not for lack of intention, but because she doesn't know you and most women are not comfortable being sexual around men they don't know. Trust takes time. She has to see that your actions line up with your intentions before she can feel comfortable exposing herself to you and making herself vulnerable.

Women have a lot more to lose from expressing their sexuality than men do. They make babies. We don't. They get raped and/or sexually assaulted at a startlingly high rate. We don't. They have five thousands years of sexist cultural history making them feel like a slut. We don't.

The second you make them feel uncomfortable sexually is the second you become a creep and the second she's finding an excuse to get away from you as fast as she can.

This is why vulnerability is so huge. When you're vulnerable around someone you don't know, it elicits trust in them and they will become more vulnerable toward you in return. The more vulnerable a woman is willing to be around you, the less likely you will be to creep her out.

(Caveat 1: Vulnerability is still subject to the right intentions. If you tell a girl a sob story for no other reason than to get her to feel sorry for you and sleep with you, then guess what, you're still creepy!)

(Caveat 2: Sex can be viewed as the ultimate act of vulnerability for a woman. The more vulnerable you make yourself around her — by leading, by sharing your intentions, by being honest — the more she will trust you and become vulnerable in return. Sex is a side effect of that mutual vulnerability.)

Paradoxically, the way to interact with women in a vulnerable way and, therefore, the way to combat creepiness, is to accept that some women will find you creepy some of the time. Just as with rejection, the more you're willing to risk it, the less it will happen.

The more comfortable you are with women finding you creepy, and the more uninhibited and vulnerable your actions and words are around women, and the more aware and respectful you are of their interests and desires, the less likely they will be to find you creepy. The more reserved and closed up you are about your intentions, the more you attempt to manipulate her and mislead her about what you want and who you are, the more you disregard her feelings and actions toward you, the more likely you are to become creepy.

Obviously, there are technical aspects of communication that affect this as well. Bad body language, strange conversation topics, uncalibrated humor, inappropriate touching — these things can all make you creepy even with the best of intentions. This is why I say that at some point you have to accept that you're going to creep some women out and that's OK. Because the alternative is to hide your sexuality and hope a woman comes to you — and well, we all know how well that works out.

Sexual Tension

Flirting is the opposite of creepiness. Flirting is expressing your sexuality in a way that makes a woman feel sexually secure.

Sometimes the sexuality of your behavior is overt, sometimes it's subtle, sometimes it's implied. But when done correctly, it's accepted and appreciated by women.

If you research dating advice and pick up tips, you'll find dozens and dozens of methods of "building attraction" with women. Some of the more popular ones include teasing, bantering, negging, cocky/funny, push/pull, qualification, statements of interest, false disqualifiers, roleplaying, leading and pacing, eliciting values, magic tricks, cold-reading, false takeaways, word games, hand games, betting and competition, etc.

Chances are, you've read or are familiar with at least a few of these concepts. If you don't know what most of them are, then good, don't worry about it. No, I'm serious — don't worry about it, because they all follow the same basic pattern.

Flirting is expressing your sexuality to a woman in a way that makes her feel secure expressing her sexuality back towards you.

In a nutshell, what a lot of men refer to as "game" is their ability to flirt with women. How well can they express their sexuality to women with positive responses? If they can do it often, they have "game."

The tactics or strategies used (teasing, etc.) all do this in their own ways, but they all follow the same pattern. For the sake of time and space (and boredom), I'll be grouping most methods of flirting into two different groups: teasing and boldness. Both teasing and bold types of flirting (whether it's negging, false takeaways, or roleplaying) follow the same basic formula: they all involve breaking rapport in order to generate sexual tension.

172

Scientific research shows that sexual tension builds when the uncertainty of potential sexual possibilities is presented in an interaction.

For example, if I say something with implied sexual innuendo like, "Well, that's cool you are into cats, maybe I can come over and play with your pussy for a while," this generates sexual tension because, assuming she doesn't throw her drink in my face or slap me, it leaves the possibility of a future sexual encounter on the table. It's a story with no ending, the human brain wants to know what happens next. And in this case, what happens next is probably something sexual.

Teasing type behaviors generate sexual tension because they generate uncertainty as to whether or not you're actually interested in a woman. In the example above, depending on the context and situation, I could be totally joking and being facetious. Or I could be totally serious and masking my desires behind a thinly-veiled joke. She doesn't know. And that's what makes it so good. The uncertainty generates the tension.

If you tease a woman about her hair, telling her she looks like ET with a perm, or that your grandmother once owned a wig like that, you accomplish sexual tension because you are sending mixed signals. Your intentions are sending a "Yes, I like you," signal, while your words are sending a, "No, I don't," signal. This generates uncertainty and, therefore, sexual tension.

This is why most dating advice in western culture, to both men *and* women, encourages you to send mixed messages, "play hard to get," or play games with one another. Sure, it distorts intentions, but it also generates uncertainty and therefore, sexual tension.

But one can flirt by being clear with one's intentions as well. One can state one's sexual desires clearly or actually even move to make those sexual desires happen. It's counterintuitive, but this can generate a lot of uncertainty and sexual tension as well.

For instance, let's say you meet a woman and just come right out and say, "I think you're beautiful, I'd like to take you on a date."

A lot of men cringe at this idea. Needy men hate it because they think it will make them creepy. Narcissistic men hate it because they believe they're giving their power away.

But in reality, it's one of the most powerful and practical things you can say. Not only is it vulnerable, as we've discussed at length, but it also builds far more sexual tension.

But how? If she already knows you like her, how can it build tension? There's no uncertainty.

Oh, but there is. It's just not immediately obvious. Observe:

1. First of all, a direct statement like that is polarizing. So if a woman is not interested in you, she will let you know then and there. If she is interested in you, this bold statement will make her so excited that you will also know then and there. Either way, you win.

2. Women are turned on by being desired, remember? They are aroused by men who perform bold behaviors towards them. So it turns her on.

3. It also demonstrates that you are not needy, which makes you more attractive to her.

4. So now we have an aroused woman who is interested, and an attractive man who is bold and vulnerable. And both have implicitly or explicitly suggested sexual interest. Suddenly this opens up all sorts of new questions and opportunities: What is going to happen next? He's so bold and direct, I have no idea what he'll say or do. Does he want to kiss me? Does he want to fuck me? Do I want to fuck him? I do and I don't. I don't know what to do. When is he going to touch me? What will it be like? Will I love it?

See, if a man is having an innocuous conversation with a bunch of small talk, there is never any uncertainty in the woman's mind as to where things stand. The conversation is shallow and simple and so there's no question as to why they're talking or the significance of what they're talking about.

If a man begins to flirt with a woman by teasing her, then suddenly he adds a new dimension by creating uncertainty: Does he like me or not? Why is he flirting with me?

But if a man goes the bold and vulnerable route, and is willing to risk rejection, he is rewarded by creating massive amounts of sexual tension,

174

because in a single stroke you have transported the context away from, "What do we talk about next?" to "What will he say or do with me next?"

This is extremely powerful.

Of course, this is often easier said than done. Flirting this way requires showing vulnerability, risking rejection, and/or potentially being creepy. And at first, you may flirt in needy and supplicant ways, repelling women even faster than you did when you were just plain and boring. But eventually, exposing yourself and your sexual desires will force you to be less invested, more confident, more dominant, and more attractive. The teasing will help by creating the perception of non-neediness, and the boldness will make women more and more receptive to your eventual sexual advances.

But unlike fears of living an attractive lifestyle, flirting and expressing your sexuality requires communicating effectively. It requires competency at certain social behaviors. And social behaviors, like any other kind of behavior, aren't simply picked up overnight. They must be built and honed through practice.

Developing an Emotional Connection

Your ability to connect with a woman emotionally is proportional to how self-aware you are of your own emotional processes and motivations.

As described in Chapter 2, self-awareness and vulnerability will cause you to behave in a less needy manner, they give her the chance to know the "real you," to trust you, and to open her own emotions up to you.

Ultimately, this is what most women want. If you look at romance novels — basically the female version of porn — they all follow more or less the exact same pattern: hard and rugged bad-boy type male hero is troubled but strong, and as he slowly opens up and shares his true emotions and desires with the heroine, she's able to support him, to save him and ultimately fall in love with him. Of course, they live happily ever after.

This is more or less the blueprint of seduction: a strong, high status, attractive exterior (lifestyle and looks), fearless, and able to open up and share your vulnerable side with her. Women get weak in the knees for this shit. And it's not even conscious most of the time.

175

All that's required is a certain level of emotional self-awareness and vulnerability in your interactions.

And let me tell you, emotional connections are *powerful*. Far more powerful than any sort of tactics or tricks you may learn in other books. When you connect with women emotionally, they really open up to you in ways that you can't imagine, your interactions and relationships with them become these rich and unique experiences that can never be replicated, the sex is far better, and all mind games, flakes and ambivalence goes out the window.

A lot of pick up and dating advice is what I call "attraction obsessed." It has a constant, incessant harping on being the most attractive/alpha guy possible — usually by employing all sorts of tricks, games, tactics, techniques, manipulation and other falsehoods. Attraction obsession comes from a place of insecurity. It seeks validation. It's needy behavior and, therefore, self-sabotaging in the long run.

It's not about attraction. She's attracted to men all the time but doesn't sleep with any of them or date them. Women actually don't sleep with most men they're attracted to because they would feel slutty or cheap.

Her feeling slutty or cheap isn't about an "Oh, I put out on a first date," thing. It's not about number of dates, hours spent together, or how many dinners you bought her.

Feeling slutty is about sleeping with a man who doesn't care about her or who hasn't connected with her. If she doesn't trust you or isn't 100% convinced that you really like her and care about her, then she's not going to do it. And if she does, then she'll regret it and feel dirty.

So how do you develop deep and lasting emotional connections with women, connections that will blow your mind and heart away as well as hers too? Connections that will give you some of the best nights and sex of your life?

Glad you asked.

Here's the basic pattern, and you should recognize a lot of overlap here with Chapter 2:

   - Becoming aware of your own emotions, motivations, and life story.

- Taking the lead by sharing those emotions, motivations, and life story first.
- Sharing first creates trust and encourages her to open up and share herself in return.
- Ideally, the more this goes on, the more personal the stories become and the deeper the emotions are by which you connect.

For instance, take a simple conversation about music you two like. She likes Empire of the Sun. You like Empire of the Sun. Instead of just saying, "I really like Empire of the Sun," you can expand and talk about *why* you like Empire of the Sun.

Instead of just, "I like Empire of the Sun," you could say, "I love Empire of the Sun. They always remind me of my brother. My brother used to drive me to school for years, and he would blast Empire of the Sun every morning. Looking back, it meant a lot to me, my brother taking care of me like that. My dad was always too busy. So Empire of the Sun always reminds me of that. Those moments of appreciation that you don't recognize until years later."

Wow, that's a little intense, right? That's the idea. If you feel uncomfortable just reading that and imagining yourself saying something like it, then that's good. That's vulnerability. And ultimately, that's what's going to make you an attractive man who can emotionally connect with women.

Things can go even deeper as well. For instance, it's one thing to talk about jobs. Maybe she's a lawyer and came from a poor immigrant background. It may be obvious that she worked very hard and is very ambitious. You could relate to that by sharing how when you were a teenager, a couple of your best friends were injured in a car accident and how that affected you, scared you straight, and helped you become grateful for every day you have, how you started taking advantage of your time and potential and worked very hard to get where you are.

Whatever it is, open up about it. Challenge yourself to go one level deeper.

And the most important rule of emotional connection is to relate to feelings, not facts. Seduction is about feelings, not facts. This is why you can often meet a woman who shares a *lot* in common with you — same home town, same occupation, same interests, lives on the same street — and have no connection or chemistry whatsoever. But then you can meet a woman who has lived an entirely different life from you, but if you can relate to the emotional struggles and emotional realities that she's gone through, you can connect deeply with her.

She may be a rich girl whose father died when she was eight and who was sent to boarding school, and you may have had to work your way up from poverty in India and then move to the USA, but emotionally, you can relate very deeply — the alienation from home, growing up with no sense of family or support other than achievement, feeling isolated by your talent.

Everybody on this planet shares a handful of universal emotional realities: ambition, shame, alienation, loneliness, achievement, regret, hardship, friendship, love, heartbreak. We've all experienced it. The facts change, the feelings are the same. I don't care how shallow or dumb or weird or annoying she is, she has it somewhere in her. It's your job to dig it out and connect with it. That's where the gold is. That's where the real magic happens. Challenge yourself to find it. Because once you do, you'll never go back.

And the biggest misconception about generating a strong emotional connection is that it obligates you to some sort of commitment. It doesn't. Although it's more likely to cause you two to want to commit to one another, a relationship commitment is an intellectual construct, emotional connection happens organically on an unconscious level.

Be careful though, some women *will* feel cheated if you get too close to them without following through on any sort of commitment. Our culture has hammered it into women's head that emotion equals commitment equals happily-ever-after, but that's just rarely the case. So make sure when you connect with women on a deep level, they can handle it — that they're conscious enough to understand your expectations and that just because you feel a lot with each other, you're not necessarily obligated to one another.

Building and Breaking Habits

Your communication skills are a series of overlapping habits. You have habits that influence when and how you make eye contact with people, how you speak, your voice inflections, what kinds of questions you ask, whether you lead the conversation or follow, whether you're curious about others or self-centered, how often you smile, look away or laugh. The list goes on and on.

If you have trouble relating to people, particularly women, then chances are you've developed communication habits that are unattractive and are not serving you well.

Some of these habits are simple to learn and fix, such as making more eye contact. Others are more difficult to notice and harder to fix, for instance deferring to the opinion of others when making an observation.

The specific habits that are attractive and unattractive will be covered in the next chapter. But for now, I want to wrap up this chapter by going over the process by which you can build and break these habits.

A lot of men get the wrong idea. They'll read some dating advice saying something like, "touch her on the arm when you smile at her." Then they'll go out and do it and it'll feel very awkward and stilted, so they'll never do it again.

The reason it feels awkward and stilted is because they've never done it before. It's not a habit for them yet. In fact, *not* touching a woman when they smile is a habit, and they're trying to break it. Habits are hard to break. They take time. And you have to do them repeatedly.

The trick is to identify the good/bad habits you want to build or break and the focus on them consciously until they're second nature. This actually doesn't take a long time. For simple things such as eye contact or posture, it may only take a few weeks. For things such as touching, or making statements instead of questions, it may be even shorter.

Either way, the more you implement the habits, the better your reactions from women will be, thereby increasing your motivation to implement the habits further.

Basically, what I'm saying here, is that everything described in the next chapter is not an overnight fix, you have to go out and do it over and over again.

And just as with desensitizing yourself to your anxieties, you want to focus on one at a time, two at the most.

Another problem many men run into is that they learn that they need to make strong eye contact, lean back on their back foot, touch on the approach, make observations about her features, qualify her on her passions, smile when she smiles and touch her when she laughs *all at the same time.*

So they go out, and get completely jumbled up and don't know what to focus on and are unable to focus on all of the behaviors at the same time.

It often actually makes their interactions much worse.

We won't be doing that. In fact, I think a lot of the tiny habits listed above are overrated. I'll be presenting attractive social habits in more general terms so that 1) you have fewer things clogging your brain, and 2) there will still be room to express your personality and unique ticks.

You'll also notice that many of these habits are directly correlated with overcoming fears and anxieties as discussed in Chapters 9 and 10. For instance, developing the habit of touching a woman when you make a joke relates directly to an anxiety many men feel about showing sexual interest. The habit of smiling when you introduce yourself to somebody ties into the anxiety of meeting new people.

Many of these behaviors are linked to your anxieties. And the interesting thing is that you can resolve them from both sides: fixing your outer behaviors will help alleviate your internal anxiety, and alleviating your internal anxiety will help fix up your outer behaviors.

As always, attractive social behaviors are rooted in a comfort with making yourself vulnerable, an honest expression of your desires, and ultimately, embodying non-neediness and investing in yourself.

Chapter 12
How to Improve Your Flirting

Sometimes, even if your intentions are in line and you're expressing yourself openly, people won't always necessarily perceive you correctly. Communication is always up for interpretation; therefore, there's always going to be a chance that you'll be misunderstood or people might make incorrect judgments about you. There's also a good chance that you aren't expressing yourself *clearly* or *effectively*.

For instance, you may ask a girl out for coffee. But perhaps she's inexperienced or comes from a conservative background, and so what is a clear statement of interest from you, appears to her as just an invitation for friendship.

Or maybe you compliment a woman on her dress. But for whatever reason, your tonality, and facial expression aren't clear and she thinks you're being sarcastic. Maybe she's insecure and very touchy about men complimenting her, so she responds negatively.

In the long run, misunderstandings and miscommunications are unavoidable. No matter how clear and how charming you are there are always going to be women who misinterpret what you say to them as well as your intentions. This is a fact of life and something you have to get used to.

But what we can control is how efficiently and openly we communicate by learning clear and effective communication skills. The better our communication skills, the more clearly we can express ourselves and show sexual interest. The more clearly we express ourselves and show sexual interest, the more likely we'll be able to connect with women in a sexual and emotional way.

It's sad but true. There are often situations where a woman will be sexually interested in a man, but their failure to communicate their intentions to one another clearly will derail the entire interaction. There's no excuse to let this happen.

And as with all of the Three Fundamentals, you'll find that clear communication will enhance other areas of your life — your professional relationships, your family relationships, your friendships, your networking abilities — just as much as it enhances your romantic relationships and your ability to meet and attract women.

First Impressions

First impressions are crucial. Studies show that we base the majority of our perception of people on the first few minutes we spend with them. This initial perception can extend and influence our relationship to the person for weeks or even months.

If I look at all of the women I've dated seriously, just about all of them (I'd estimate 90% or so), it felt "on" within the first few minutes of the interaction. We clicked and that first impression led to a romantic and sexual relationship further down the line.

The biggest misconception about first impressions is being overly concerned with what to say to a woman when you meet her. What you say to her when you first meet her is actually unimportant, and hopefully by this point in the book, I don't have to explain why.

The exact words you say are far less important than your intentions and level of anxiety.

Ninety percent of the time when I meet a new woman, I simply say, "Hi, I'm Mark." I then follow it up with, "I wanted to meet you." And if I'm feeling particularly bold, I'll say, "I thought you were cute and wanted to meet you."

That's it.

You can ask a woman how her day is going, or say the most perceptive and witty thing to her in the first minutes, but her first impression is largely going to be based on how you present yourself (looks/lifestyle; Chapters 7 and 8), your level of anxiety (anxiety; Chapters 9 and 10), and your ability to communicate clearly. What actually comes out of your mouth is going to be forgotten or completely irrelevant within seconds.

With that in mind, here are guidelines for making a good first impression:

- Do *not* startle or scare her when you approach her. This is possibly the only death knell for approaching women. If you startle her or scare her when she first meets you, in my experience, there is almost absolutely nothing you can do to recover. You're immediately labeled "creepy" and she will do anything possible to get out of the situation. Even if she's polite and talks for a minute, chances are she's never going to open up and trust you.

  Typical ways guys startle or scare women upon the approach are by approaching them from behind (huge no-no), grabbing them violently, screaming at them, or saying something offensive or weird.

- When in doubt on how to approach a woman, simply walk up and introduce yourself and explain to her that you wanted to meet her. I know this sounds drab and boring. But remember, it's not about entertaining her; it's about being non-needy and expressing your genuine interest in her. During the day, I often preface the introduction by saying something like, "Excuse me, this is kind of random..." Also during the day, I usually tell them that I think they're cute.

  In my experience, the fancier and more creative guys try to get with their opening lines, the more likely they are to a) say something weird and b) come off as needy. Think about it, if you sit around for 10 minutes trying to think of what to say to a girl so that she'll like you, how is that ever not needy?

  She'll sense this. In fact, it's kind of amazing. Women really do seem to have a sixth sense about this stuff. I've noticed that the longer I hesitate and stare at a girl before I approach her, the more likely I am to be rejected. The best approaches I ever do are when I don't think about it and I spontaneously just walk up and say hello.

- Don't linger. If you linger and hover around her, it's almost guaranteed to make the approach feel awkward and forced. Imagine a straight line between you and her, and when you're ready to go, follow that straight line until you're standing right in front of her. Don't stand around and kick the dirt at your feet trying to work up the nerve right next to her.

- Smile. Always smile. Don't smile like the Joker from the Batman movies smiles. But smile like you're a nice, friendly person. A comfortable smile. Lean back. Stand up tall. Speak loudly yet clearly. Make strong eye contact. Introduce yourself and stick out your hand. Give a firm handshake. This is called being a confident human being.

If you are getting many rejections right on the initial approach, then it's one of the following three things:

1. You're presenting yourself poorly — i.e., you dress poorly, bad looks, bad style, bad body language. Review Chapters 7 and 8 again.

2. Your intentions are off. You're approaching for the wrong reasons. The wrong reasons include anything that is not, "She's cute. I want to meet her." That means, approaching for statistics, approaching for "practice," approaching to impress your friends. Approaching because you want to live up to a bunch of crap you read on the internet. These are all the *wrong* reasons to approach. When you see a beautiful woman, you should be motivated by nothing but your desire to get to know her. That's it. If you have trouble finding that motivation, refer back to the section on sexual anxiety in Chapter 9.

3. You're not following one of the guidelines above. You're startling her. You're trying too hard to be clever or interesting. Or you're doing something technically wrong (not looking her in the eye, not smiling, etc.)

Like I said, if you have everything together, you should not be getting rejected often on the opener. I've coached men who still had some major flaws (lack of confidence, poor looks, anxiety), but having them follow the guidelines above still got most of the women to at least stop and talk to them for a second.

And really that's all the opener is trying to do: stop them and get them to talk to you for a second. It's your conversation skills that get that second to turn into a minute and that minute to turn into an hour.

Conversation Skills

Developing conversation skills is a deep topic, and for the sake of this book, I'm only going to gloss over the most important aspects and the advice that's easiest to implement.

The topics that we'll cover in this section are:

- Using effective language
- Questions versus statements
- Creating endless conversation topics
- Storytelling
- Basics of emotional connection

Using Effective Language: This is the easiest "quick fix" that you can apply to your communication skills. Using effective language means saying what you mean with the fewest words possible while still maintaining your meaning and intent.

This is where being a good writer can actually help you become a good communicator. If you're saying something in four sentences that could be said in one, say it in one. If you are saying something in ten words that can be said in four, say it in four.

In conversation and communication quality always wins out over quantity. We would all rather have 30 seconds of *amazing* communication than 10 minutes of mediocre communication saying the same thing.

It also means removing "um," "uh," "ah," "like," "you know," and other fillers from your everyday speaking.

Removing all fillers 100% of the time is often impossible (I still drop an "um," or "you know," occasionally), but the more of these you remove, the more clear and coherent your speaking will be. Nothing screams a lack of sophistication like somebody who sprinkles "like" and "umm" throughout his stories constantly.
Read the following two sentences out loud:

"So, um, I guess what I'm saying is like, that I never really felt at home when I lived, uh, out there, you know, in California. The people, uh, just felt kind of like, superficial to me. And I, um, didn't like really like it a whole lot I guess."

"I never really felt at home in California. The people felt kind of superficial to me. I didn't really like it."

Notice the difference in the two, notice how the second feels much more impactful and to-the-point.

You don't want to speak like a robot either. You can still use all of the inflections, tonality and pacing on the second sentence without having to drop "um" and "like" all the time.

When you read it, you should be able to feel an immediate difference. The first one feels very casual, lackadaisical, even lazy and uninterested. The second one feels serious, stern, powerful, and clear.

Questions versus Statements: Creating threads of conversation through statement is far more powerful than questions. This is because it assumes rapport and instantly makes conversations more personally.

For instance, if you've been talking to a woman at a bar for a few minutes, saying, "I love olives in my drink. When I was a kid I used to eat them straight out of the jar," is far more interesting than, "Do you like olives in your drink?" and waiting for her response. In fact, that question is just plain weird. But that statement is interesting, and what many women would consider "cute."

Instead of incessant questioning, you want to develop a skill called cold reading. Cold reading is a skill where you're able to intuitively "know" something about someone else without actually knowing it.

It's like being a psychic without the cheesiness.

For our purposes, cold reading is just a way of creating interesting statements rather than asking questions for information. You don't ask the question you want to know, but instead, you make a mild prediction.

Instead of asking her a question about herself, you guess the answer to your question and then state it. Here are some examples:

"Where are you from?" translates to: "You look like a California girl."

"What do you do for work?" translates to: "You seem to be a creative person. I bet your job is interesting."

"How do you guys know each other?" translates to: "You guys look like you've been friends for a long time."

In each situation, the statement makes an educated guess and engages the woman far more than any question will. Instead of asking her about herself, you're *telling* her about herself. The only thing people love more than talking about themselves is hearing about themselves. But what if you're wrong?

That's the best part! A lot of guys worry about cold reading because they're afraid to state something incorrect. This is where human nature works in our favor.

There's no failing with cold reading. With every cold read, one of three things will happen:

1. You'll be wrong, and she'll correct you.
2. You'll be wrong, and she'll ask you what made you think that.
3. You'll be right, and she'll freak out at how perceptive you are.

In the first result, she'll basically just answer the question you based your cold read on and forget that you were wrong.

In the second result, you'll be wrong, but she'll be so intrigued by your guess, that she'll create a deeper conversation thread about what you observed about her. Later in the chapter, we'll talk about the importance of creating the deepest threads possible.

In the third result, the few times you get the cold read correct, she will most likely be surprised at how perceptive you are about her. This will generate a tidal wave of rapport immediately and impress her at the same time.

Here are examples of a cold read situation with all three different responses:

Me: "You look a bit bookish. You must be a student around here."
Her: "No, I'm not. But I do love to read, though."

Me: "You look a bit bookish. You must be a student around here."
Her: "No. What made you think that? Is it my glasses? I just got them."

Me: "You look a bit bookish. You must be a student around here."
Her: "Yeah, I am! Wow, is it that obvious?"

You should cold read as much as possible. Any time you're asking a question that requires a factual answer, take a stab at the answer instead of asking.

One night, I met a girl from Chicago. I took a blind guess at which University she went to and was right. She couldn't get over "how perceptive" I was for a good five minutes. She asked me how I knew and I told her I could tell she was on the intellectual side although I figured she probably moved because the school was located in a bad part of the city. Everything was dead-on despite being educated guesses. From that point on, she engaged me completely in conversation and was more than excited to hang out with me again.

Besides that, creating conversations out of statements protects you from what I call "blanking." You know when you are talking to a woman and all the sudden the conversation dies and you have no idea what to say? You're sitting there awkwardly and the more uncomfortable you feel, the harder it is to come up with something. Eventually, you blurt out something boring like, "So… where do you live?"

Using statements can prevent this a great deal. Instead of fishing for a new conversation based on a generic question, you can simply comment about something or observe something. Never underestimate the power of non-sequiturs.

"I'm thinking about quitting drinking." "A car almost hit me on the way here tonight." "My roommate eats peanut butter and mayonnaise sandwiches. It's disgusting." "I've always wanted to visit Africa."

These will sometimes come across as random. But that's because they are — they're whatever thoughts are popping into your head at the moment. It's better to be random and interesting than predictable and boring. Don't be afraid to just blurt something out.

This works because unlike questions, statements require no investment from the other person. You can say whatever you want and there's no implicit expectation for her to generate conversation as well.

Speaking in statements in this fashion — to generate spontaneous conversation — is important in that it forces you to share yourself with her. When you simply ask a girl questions, you aren't giving any information about yourself, so it's harder for her to trust you or build rapport. But if you simply state a fact about yourself and then talk about it, you are now sharing yourself *and* giving her a chance to chime in with her input as well.

The amazing thing about speaking in statements is if you do it correctly, she will start asking *you* questions. This may not seem like a big deal, but it actually reorients the entire interaction. As I mentioned earlier, whoever is asking the questions is sub-communicating a desire to learn more about the other, i.e., interest, i.e., they're attracted to them. If she is constantly seeking information from you, you now have the power to control the interaction — you control the information and the conversation.

Endless Conversation Topics: In every topic of conversation, there are countless opportunities to jump off onto other topics — there are countless word associations to be made.

For instance, let's assume you're talking to a woman and she says, "I never liked that restaurant. I went there on my birthday last year, and I don't remember anything past midnight. I woke up on my friend's kitchen floor."

This is loaded with opportunities to take the conversation in new directions. You could relate and talk about any of the following:

1. The restaurant she doesn't like.
2. What you did on your last birthday.
3. The last time you got black out drunk.
4. A story about waking up somewhere unusual.

Any and all of these topics will be relevant and interesting to the conversation.

If you don't already do this, it's a habit you need to ingrain in yourself — just as the comedians ingrain off-the-wall word associations.

Here are a series of examples of statements that women may make. In them, I have underlined the "jump off" points. Think of them as intersections where you can choose which direction to move the conversation. As you read through these examples, try to come up with a statement to relate to each jump off point. This will help teach you to be prepared to speak about any topic on the spot.

1. "I go to Harvard right now. But I want to move back out west. The weather's too cold up here."

2. "I'm here with <u>my friends Steve and Carrie</u>. They've been <u>dating for six months</u>, but they <u>fight like a married couple</u>."

3. "<u>We work together downtown</u> in the district. It's all right, but I'm looking to <u>change careers</u>."

4. "We were at this <u>party last night</u>. It was crazy. The <u>cops ended up busting it</u> and some <u>drunken kid got arrested</u>."

Try re-reading through these examples and at each underlined word or phrase, try to immediately come up with a thought or response about it. For example, I see Harvard, and I think of how one time I visited there and their campus looks like a palace. I also think of friends of mine who went to Harvard. These are both legitimate places to take the conversation.

Once you become competent at this, you'll notice that this is the way in which every conversation flows. Conversations only end when one person says something to which the other person has no jump off points. This is what happens when a conversation "dies." If you teach yourself to recognize jump off points and take advantage of them as soon as possible, you'll be able to sustain a conversation with almost anybody indefinitely.

Combine this skill with the ability to cold read and create conversational threads out of thin air by making statements, and you will literally develop the skill to begin and control any conversation with anybody for any length of time.

Storytelling. Human beings, by default, are enrapt by stories, or more specifically, a story arc. Politicians use them to campaign, teachers use them to explain important concepts, comedians use them to make us laugh, and we use them constantly in our day-to-day interactions.

But what you probably didn't notice is that the best communicators you know are fantastic storytellers.

Have you ever had a friend who would start telling you about something and it just seemed to go nowhere? Like, they'd start telling you about their trip to Chicago and after describing the hotel and maybe mentioning the concierge, the story just died?

Or have you ever known someone who consistently makes jokes that don't completely make sense, or fizzle out and aren't funny?

Or maybe you're one of these people. Do people ever stop paying attention to you mid-story? Or do you have trouble making others laugh (intentionally, that is)?

Chances are, these people (or you), aren't following a strong story arc. For whatever reason, humans have evolved to be absolutely fascinated when information is communicated in a certain pattern. This is true of just about any culture and background.

There are three main points of a story arc:

Set Up: The set up is exactly that: you're setting the scene or the context for what you're about to say. It's the foundation of what's about to be told, and if you don't set up properly, then your stories, jokes, and ideas will always seem to be random. People will consistently comment that you're really random, weird, or "off the wall."

Content/Conflict: After setting up what you're going to talk about, you get into the actual content. This can also be the "conflict" in your story. Whatever it is, it's something that causes tension and expectancy. The content of your story needs to be intriguing and hook people into wanting to know what will happen next. If you don't build much tension with the content of your stories, you will find people losing interest or get the feeling like you ramble on a lot.

Resolution: The resolution releases the tension from the conflict or content. Resolutions can come in forms of punchlines (for jokes), conclusions (for ideas), or just closure for a generic story. People who don't resolve their stories and ideas well will often get blank stares when they're finished speaking, or people asking them, "Yeah, and...?" not realizing that the story is finished.

Here's an example of a story with a setup, content/conflict, and a resolution:

> When I was in college, my first roommate had a funny habit whenever he got drunk. He'd basically turn into a narcoleptic — he'd spontaneously fall asleep in strange places and at random moments (Setup).
>
> Well, literally the first night I knew this guy, he and I go out to some orientation party. We meet a couple girls and go back to their dorm with them. He and I are totally drunk and I notice he's kind of

stopped talking to his girl and is dozing off in the corner. Kind of weird, but it was like 3 AM, so whatever. Suddenly, he says he's going to go and gets up and leaves. I think nothing of it until I go home, wake up the next morning and he's still not back. Hours pass and I start getting worried (Content/Conflict).

It turns out that the guy went out into the hallway lobby, laid down on the floor and slept there the whole night. But not only that, he left his jacket in the girl's room. So at like 9 in the morning he had to sneak back in, wake her up and take his jacket back. It was pretty hilarious at the time. But yeah, that was my college roommate (Resolution).

Often adding a line like, "Yeah, that was my college roommate," is good because it indicates that the story is finished and that you're finished speaking.

Here's another example:

I knew I wasn't meant for the 9 to 5 world almost immediately. Out of college, I took a nice job at a prestigious bank in downtown Boston (Setup).

I hated it from day one. In fact, I remember thinking about three hours into the first day, "I wonder how long I have to work here before I can leave?" (Conflict/Content).

My next thought was, "This is probably a bad sign." (Resolution).

Notice that I allude to the conclusion in the beginning of my story. This is called "foreshadowing" and often helps people follow along. Also, notice that it really doesn't matter how long or short each component of the story is as long as you convey the correct information.

Another example:

When most people talk about a crazy city, I don't think they've ever been to South America. I lived down there for a few months last Spring and you see things every week that are just beyond our reality here (Setup).

Like one night, we hopped in a cab to go to another nightclub. It was a Tuesday at about 4 AM. The taxi driver promptly turns around and asks us if we'd like to try some of his cocaine. We politely refuse. So the cabbie says in Spanish, "Fine, more for me." He then proceeds to do lines of coke while driving 50mph with his knees (Content/Conflict).

We all thought we were going to die that night (Resolution).

All true stories by the way…

In the last section, we talked about "jump off points" in conversation and how that's how we learn to relate to one another. The examples showed jump off points in individual sentences.

In real life, people speak in more than sentences; they speak to each other in stories. So you'll want to develop the ability to formulate entire *stories* around jump off points, as well as notice jump off points within entire stories.

This is actually much easier than it sounds, and you probably do it naturally with your friends and family in a lot of situations. The idea is to just do it consistently and naturally and with anybody, including attractive women.

Relating and Connecting. The final goal of a successful conversation is to actually make a personal connection with the woman you're talking to.

When you are talking to a woman, there are only two *real* subjects of conversation: her and you. Everything you speak about should be, in some way, revealing your identity to her or her identity to you.

This uncovering of identity is what creates the sense of a "connection." The greater the connection you create, the more she'll want to spend time with you and vice-versa.

Making a connection requires three steps: 1) being open about yourself, 2) getting her to be open about herself, and 3) relating to each other's experiences.

So what do you talk about? How do you talk about yourself openly? When I tell guys "talk about yourself more. Open up." A lot of them go out and say, "I'm from New York. I like baseball. I'm 27." It's good that they're sharing themselves now, but that's a bit shallow.

Take out a sheet of paper and write down three things for each of the following:

- Your passions and favorite things to do.
- Your dreams, ambitions, life goals.
- The best/worst things that have happened to you.
- Your childhood, family life, and upbringing.

Now, go back to each item you wrote down and talk about it to yourself for one minute. Try to be as detailed and honest as possible.
It's not as easy as it sounds. Even when you're alone sometimes talking about these subjects makes you a little uneasy.

Most men feel a bit vulnerable when talking about these topics, especially to women. That's the point.

Be willing to share any part of yourself to anyone at any time and on any level. You have nothing to lose by sharing yourself. At the worst, she'll reject you and, well, she's going to reject you if all you do is talk about sports and your job anyway, so what's the problem?

What you'll actually find is when you share something deeper and personal about yourself, it will be genuine and she'll immediately respond to that by being genuine herself.

Ideally, sharing these aspects of yourself will encourage her to share them in herself. You want to get her to talk about her passions, her ambitions, her best experiences and her most vulnerable experiences. These are the topics that define us as humans and make us unique — that is, different from the last 20 guys who talked to her.

These are the topics of conversation that will make you stand out. Why? Because she knows you. Not your favorite sports team. Not the party you went to last week, but you.

And when she knows you and remembers you, she'll make sure to pick up the phone when you call and meet up with you again.

In conclusion: When it comes to conversations, there's a lot to cover. Reading this last section may have been overwhelming for you. If so, just remember: break it up into little chunks, practice one thing at a time.

But now that we've covered how to hold a dynamic and interesting conversation, let's talk about how to spice it up. Let's talk about humor.

Humor

There's an old saying, if you can make a woman laugh then you can get her to laugh right into bed. Now, although humor is not a cure-all for anybody's dating problems, it's definitely important. In fact, in many surveys of what women look for most in a man, "sense of humor" is almost always at the top of that list.

The reason is that a strong sense of humor conveys all of the attractive traits of your identity to a woman. A man who can laugh easily at the world and who isn't afraid to laugh at himself conveys a sense of non-neediness. He also makes women feel good around him and, therefore, more secure. A man who is very serious and unable to laugh at himself or the world conveys that he is heavily invested in the perceptions of the world around him and is therefore needy.

Your specific type of sense of humor isn't so important as much as that you have it. Obviously, different women will respond strongly to different types of humor, but this is less a function of your ability to tell jokes and more a function of demographics. Sarcastic women will like sarcastic men. Silly women will like silly men, and so on. Focus on what you find funny to you personally, and don't be afraid to share that with the women you meet. If they laugh, then great! If they don't, then chances are it wasn't going to work anyway.

At its core, humor is the art of drawing connections between two seemingly unrelated ideas or objects. There are a number of ways to do this, but at its core, humor is a *creative activity* and, therefore, will greatly be tied to your ability to uninhibitedly express yourself.

Sometimes your jokes will fall flat, particularly when you're starting out. That's OK. Don't laugh at yourself. Don't make fun of yourself. Don't try to explain the joke. These are all needy responses that are dependent on others' perceptions of yourself rather than your own. Sometimes jokes are bad or unfunny. That's fine. Just move on.

In this section, I'll give a brief overview of a few types of humor: misdirection, exaggeration, sarcasm, wordplay, and roleplaying.

Misdirection: One of the most common and easiest forms of humor is misdirection. Misdirection occurs when you begin to say something or tell a story that leads the listener to believe you're making one point, and then out of nowhere you say something completely different. For instance, here's a famous line by Steve Martin:

"You know that look women get when they want to have sex? ... Yeah, me neither."

The line sets you up to believe that he's going to tell you a story about the time a woman gave him a look like she wanted to have sex with him. But he misdirects you and ends up making a joke about his own sexual inexperience. Here's another one from Jimmy Fallon:

"There's a new book out called 'Why Women Have Sex' that says there are 237 reasons why women have sex. And folks, David Letterman knows the top 10."

Again, he sets up the joke by telling you about a new book out relating to why women have sex. But he then takes the idea of there being 237 reasons why women have sex and relates it to David Letterman's famous "Top 10" segments on his show and the fact that Letterman got caught sleeping with his interns. It's the connection of these two seemingly unrelated topics that makes it funny.

Exaggeration: Exaggeration is another mainstay of humor and something that everyone should be able to use. Exaggeration is when you take a quality about something, and blow it completely out of proportion, often in a creative or interesting way. For instance:

"She's a nice woman, though. Nicest three acres of flesh I've ever met."

Obviously, no woman actually has three acres worth of flesh. But the exaggeration of her being fat is what causes this line to be funny. There's also a subtle misdirection in the line (going from "she's nice" to "she's fat").

Typically, the more creative and extreme you are in describing your exaggeration, the funnier it will be. For instance, notice the difference in how funny the following two lines are:

"She was as ugly as a dog."

"I've seen more attractive things in the bottom of an airport urinal."

Notice the second one is far more extreme and creative. The completely unrelated ideas of an airport urinal and a girl's face (I'm laughing just typing this) is what creates the greater degree of humor.

In humor, the more specific and odd the details, typically the more funny a joke is.

Teasing and Sarcasm. Whereas misdirection and exaggeration are funny to just about anybody, you'll run into a minority of women who don't find teasing or sarcasm funny. Teasing and sarcasm can also vary in degrees of appropriateness, especially depending on where you are. If you're at a funeral, it's probably not a good idea to make sarcastic comments about the deceased's family.

Teasing is when you make humorous comments that are derogatory about someone. Generally, teasing is done in good humor and with good intentions. Teasing with bad intentions becomes insulting and is not welcome by most people.

Teasing is supposed to be fun. The ideal tease will create a mixture of emotions in a girl: defensiveness yet happiness. The ideal reaction is when a girl will say, "Oh my god, I can't believe you said that," but will be laughing at the same time and smiling. Here are a couple examples of teases:

> (To a woman wearing bright red shoes)
>
> *"Are you going to click your heels to go home later?"*
>
> (To a woman sitting by herself in the corner looking bored)
>
> *"So who put you in timeout?"*
>
> (To a woman waving a dollar bill at the bartender to get his attention)
>
> *"Is that how you always get men to pay attention to you?"*

Be careful with teases, especially to women you don't know. I said the last one to a woman I didn't know and got slapped. Then again, I still slept with her, but when you tease frequently and freely, be prepared for a wide range of emotional responses. Teasing polarizes, often hard and quickly. Therefore, it's a good tactic, but not always exactly pleasant.

Sometimes girls will genuinely be offended or sensitive to teasing and not react well. I'd say maybe 1/3 of the women I meet do not react well to teasing or a good-natured ribbing. Make a point to spot these women and let the teasing go. Generally women who don't enjoy being teased really appreciate genuine compliments, so I switch it up.

Sarcasm is an even darker form of humor than teasing. Sarcasm works on even fewer women, but the women who appreciate it really appreciate it. Chances are a lot of you reading this don't have a very sarcastic sense of humor. That's fine. You can just live a sexless and lonely life forever.

(That was sarcasm if you missed it.)

Seriously, sarcasm isn't for everybody. Sarcasm is when you make an extreme statement that's completely opposite of what you actually mean. You often say it with complete seriousness and without smiling.

A lot of women won't get sarcastic humor. They'll think you're being serious or they'll get confused. Others don't enjoy it very much. But I will say, in my experience, when a woman loves sarcasm, she *loves* sarcasm.

Years ago, I was out with a girl at a bar. We had been flirting all night and she had a very sarcastic sense of humor. At one point she looked at my drink and said, "You drink slow, I've already finished my drink!"

I replied with a totally straight face, "Not all of us hate ourselves as much as you do."

She nearly fell over laughing. She loved it and we ended up having a great relationship together.

The Role of Swearing. Swearing and dirty language has an interesting role in humor. Many types of humor, such as sarcasm and exaggeration require a certain level of edginess to pack a powerful punch.

Using dirty language or swear words is kind of a cheap and easy way to make whatever you say more extreme. For instance, adding the word "fucking" into just about any humorous statement will make it pack a little more of a punch.

At the same time, using swear words is kind of a shortcut, and if you use them too often, they'll get old quickly and sound try-hard. Dropping a well-timed F-bomb can make a funny joke even funnier. But dropping an F-bomb into everything you say just makes you look unsophisticated.

Generally, the older you are, the more I recommend avoiding dirty language. Use it sparingly and only use it when you have a specific reason to. The more you use it, the more attention-seeking and negative you will make yourself appear, both of which are unattractive traits.

Wordplay and Puns: Wordplay is similar to misdirection in that the listener expects one type of meaning and gets another, but wordplay practices misdirection by using words that have various meanings.

A few examples:

> *"Hurry, a passenger is ill. We need to get to a hospital."*
> *"What is it?"*
>
> *"It's a building with lots of doctors. But we don't have time for that."*

Or:

> *"Surely, you can't be serious!"*
>
> *"I am serious. And please, don't call me Shirley."*

I would say that puns and wordplay are an even rarer form of appreciated humor than sarcasm. Puns and wordplay also tend to be very intellectual. You'll find few women who appreciate them. And chances are even fewer of you reading this like to say them. But again, when you do find a woman who appreciates them, in my experience she really appreciates them.

Roleplaying and Games: Games and roleplaying are quick and easy ways to inject fun into any interaction with a woman. They're playful. And they open up plenty of opportunities for other types of humor when you use them.

Games can be anything from basic physical games (hand slaps, thumb wars, etc.) to word games (five questions game, fuck/marry/kill, etc.). For instance, fuck/marry/kill is easy. You point to three random people in the room and you say, "OK, out of those three people, who would you fuck, who would marry, and who would you kill, and why?"

This game can lead to quite of bit of interesting conversation based on people watching.

Roleplaying can be just as energizing and fun. Roleplaying basically involves giving the woman you're talking to a fake role and then playing around with that role. Some of my favorite roleplaying involves marriage/divorce roleplaying.

For instance, when I first meet a girl, let's say within 30 seconds she says something I don't like. I'll say, "That's it, we're getting divorced." It's funny because I just met her, but you can actually milk a lot of fun out of something simple like this — for example, "You keep the kids, I'm moving to Europe." "By the way, your music sucks, and I never liked your casseroles either."

If you find yourself having a lot of trouble with humor, I recommend watching a lot of stand-up comedians. Some of my favorites are Louis CK, George Carlin, and Bill Hicks. Pay attention to their delivery, their timing, and their facial expressions. These things can't be taught in a book, so pay attention to them. Pick a few of your favorite comics and watch their stand-up routines multiple times to get a real sense of how they tell a story and how they nail a punchline.

Also, beware of falling into the trap of self-deprecating humor. A lot of men, particularly needy men who are highly invested in other people's reactions around them, will make fun of themselves and put themselves down in order to get a laugh.

Although this may make women laugh, when used in excess, it's a needy behavior because you're sacrificing your own self-perception for the sake of others' amusement. Therefore, it's ultimately unattractive. Guys with a good sense of humor who habitually use it on themselves, I recommend turning those same jokes and thoughts onto the women you're talking to. Instead of making fun of yourself, make fun of her. It may feel uncomfortable at first, but you'll be surprised at how it will blow your interactions wide open and infuse more sexuality and playfulness into them.

Humor is not a cure-all for your problems with attracting and seducing women (if there were a cure-all, it'd be physicality; Chapter 14). Some naturally funny men overly rely on their ability to make a girl laugh and actually overdo it. Instead of being attractive and strong men, they become entertainers constantly seeking attention and validation. The worst part about this habit is that it all happens while making the woman laugh and making her enjoy your company. So a lot of men get confused and actually think that they're seducing her. She's smiling. She's laughing. She likes me. She must be sexually attracted to me, right?

Sadly, no. Humor is only useful if used in conjunction with leading her in a dominant manner and pushing things physically with her. Ultimately, you aren't ever *really* attracting a woman unless you're connecting with her physically and emotionally. And although humor is a very useful tool to help you do that, it doesn't actually do it for you.

Chapter 13
The Dating Process

Like it or not, the dating process follows a somewhat rigid line. Boy meets girl, asks girl on date, corresponds with girl, sets up date with girl, corresponds with girl, sets up second date with girl, repeat until eventually you bring girl home with you, and at some point you decide if you're exclusive, non-exclusive, a casual couple, fuck buddies, soul-mates, or never want to see each other ever again.

There are exceptions to this process, and the process can be sped up to a degree, but more or less, there's a courtship process that we all follow. Our culture has silently defined a procedure for these things, and any man who wishes to be successful with women needs to be aware of the procedure.

The process almost always involves the following: trading of contact details, talking through text or phone conversations, going on dates, sex, and figuring out what kind of relationship (if any) will result. Usually (but not always) in that order. In certain instances, the contact details and date can be forgone and you can bring her home (or go home with her) the day/night you meet her. But these cases are rare and usually involve meeting a woman in a party or nightclub situation which we won't get into a whole lot of depth about.

Phone Numbers

There's a minor obsession in men's dating advice about phone numbers, correspondence, and so-called "text game" or "flake prevention."

Flaking is a term often used to describe a woman who gives you her phone number, says she wants to see you again, and then either never responds or returns your call, or never shows up on a date. Flakes can simply be women who never respond to you or women who respond but keep sidestepping meeting up with you.

Obsessing about flakes and how to win them over is an easy trap to fall into. But in my opinion, this is treating the symptom, not the illness.

The way to prevent flakes is to meet and attract women who are so interested in you that they would never consider flaking.

Problem solved.

In my experience, 99% of the so-called flake prevention strategies guys implement — calling at certain times, baiting with open-ended texts, pretending to send a text to the "wrong person" — these will rarely convince a girl who was never attracted to you to suddenly become attracted to you. And even if by some chance they do convince her to meet up with you, you're now on a date with a woman who has no genuine interest being there with you.

Similarly, men spend way too much time obsessing over unimportant details like how many times to text each day, how soon to call her, when to ask her out, etc. Setting rigid rules such as "wait three days to ask her out" or "never text her twice in a row," greatly limits you and will hinder the unique connection you spent your time developing with the woman. And by the way, it's that connection that's going to get her out to see you again, not the clever text you spent 45 minutes coming up with.

But with that said, here is my version of "The Rules" to calling and texting women:

- Only ask a woman for her phone number if she seems genuinely attracted and interested in you. Only ask for her number if you can see yourself wanting to hang out with her again or having time to hang out with her again. If you meet a girl who is in town for a bachelorette party for three days, is drunk, and you have a serious meeting at work in two days, don't bother.

- When you ask her for her phone number, don't come up with a fancy line or make up a reason. Just ask her for it. If you're attracted to her, you shouldn't be afraid to hide it (you're a confident, dominant man, remember?). If she's attracted to you, she'll be more than excited to give it to you. Most women will always give you their number when you ask. Even if they don't like you or have no intention of ever seeing you again, they'll give it to you. It's simply far easier for them to ignore calls from guys they don't like than to reject every guy to their face.

- Flakes happen to everybody. Get used to it. There are simply too many things going on in most attractive women's lives to figure out why each one flakes. It could be because her ex-boyfriend started calling her again. It could be because she met her soul mate the day after she met you. It could be because she got in a freak accident and is in the hospital. It could be because she got sick and was bed-ridden. Sometimes women just don't feel like dating for a while. Sometimes they don't remember you well because they were drunk when they met you. Sometimes they lose their phone. Sometimes they just change their mind the next day. And sometimes they just don't care enough.

There are a million legitimate reasons women can flake other than then not being attracted to you. Trying to figure out which ones are flaking for legitimate reasons and which ones are not is more or less an impossible task. You're better off just letting it go and moving on. In the end, it comes down to the fact that if she likes you enough, she'll find a way to make it happen. If she's not finding a way to make it happen, then she probably doesn't like you as much as you thought she did.

Think of it this way. If Brad Pitt texted her asking her out, do you think she could suddenly clear her busy work schedule and move her weekend plans back? I think so. If she's not doing that for you, then she's just not that interested.

- My policy with flakes is "Three strikes you're out." If a woman flakes once, I'll try her a second time. If she doesn't respond the second time, I may or may not give it a third shot, but typically if I do, I don't put much effort into the third attempt. Often I will only try a woman once or twice. If there's still nothing after the third attempt, I move on.

A lot of women will give you excuses why they can't meet up, cancel dates, push dates back, or simply stop responding. Sometimes they have legitimate reasons. Sometimes they're making excuses. This is why at the first reason they give, I always give them the benefit of the doubt and try again. The second time, if I'm particularly interested in them and/or I think they genuinely have had two legitimate excuses, I will try them one more time. Often I will even tell them, "OK, last chance though." After the third try, I just let them go. It's not worth the time or effort at that point.

- I always text within 24 hours of getting her number. I send a simple text: "Hey Sara, it was nice meeting you." That's it. Most girls who are interested in you will respond somewhat quickly. The ones who do not respond to this will usually flake on you.

- From there, I usually wait another day or so and start a text conversation. I like to reference a conversation we had when we met in this text to try and keep some continuity. The goal here is nothing special, just trying to get a little bit of back and forth going. It's been over 24 hours and I'm seeing how warm the lead still is. Typically, if I can get a text conversation going here, then she's pretty likely to go on a date with me. If her responses are few and far between, then she's likely a flake.

  Don't get fancy and try to re-invent the wheel here. Don't get cute or try to win her over if she's not responding very much. Your legwork was put in when you met her, now you're stuck with what you earned. I've found that the cuter or harder you try to win girls over by text, the bigger chance you have of looking needy and desperate and losing them.

  Joke and tease her if she's being responsive. If she's not, stick to trying to get her out ASAP.

- Depending how the text conversation goes, I'll either ask her out right then and there, or I'll wait another day or two depending on my schedule. It used to be expected that you call women, but texting has quickly overtaken phone calls. Back in 2005 when I started this stuff, I called every number I got. Now I almost never call a girl unless she specifically asks that I call her. I would say in the last year, over 90% of my dates have been set up through texting.

- I have to say this again: don't get fancy or cute in your texts. Texting is, in general, an awful medium for communication. Often if you try to get too sarcastic or witty in your texts, they can be easily misinterpreted or come off with a completely different intention than you originally had. And remember, everything comes back to intention. So clear, blunt language. I tell guys that I only use texting to organize when she and I are going to see each other next. Literally, that's what 90% of my texts consist of, things like, "Hey, what are you doing Thursday night?" or "I'm busy this weekend, but I want to see you again."

My text conversations are boring. Just to give you an example of a typical text conversation, I've posted a transcript below of the texting I did with the last girl I went out on a date with.

Some background first: this was a girl I met in a nightclub at about 1 AM and spent no more than 60-90 minutes with. There was light kissing, but mostly just talking and dancing. No drinking (this is a biggie actually). And before she went home I mentioned that I'd like to see her the next day. She said sure.

> Me: Hey Mary, it was nice meeting you tonight.
> Her: You too! :)
> Me (next day): Hey, you said you work until 4 PM, right?
> Her: Yes, do you still want to meet?
> Me: Yeah. How about 7:30?
> Her: Can we do 8?
> Me: Sure. In the city center?
> Her: Yes, in front of the X restaurant. Do you know where it is?
> Me: Yea, see you there.
> Her: See you soon. :)

That's it. I'd say 75% of my text correspondence looks like that.

But just to show you the other extreme, here's a more unusual text transcript I had with a girl in England a few months ago. This is about as "gamey" as I ever get.

> Me: Hey Natalie, it was nice meeting you tonight.
> Her: Hey, I have your phone number now. ;)
> Me: Good, talk to you soon.
> Me (next day): Hey Natalie, how was the rest of your night?
> Her: Great. We were tired and went back a bit early though.
> Me: Good. Are you free tomorrow evening? Let's meet up for a drink.
> Her: OK. When did you have in mind?
> Me: How about 8 at X, do you know it?
> Her: Yes I do. 8 it is. I'll text you tomorrow. Good night.
> Me: Good night.
> Her (next day): Hey, I'm overloaded at work and may not be able to meet you tonight. Sorry. I hope you enjoy England.

Me: Come on Natalie. When you're old and grey are you going to wish you worked more or wish you went on more dates with cute American boys?
Her: Haha! Very true. Let me see what I can do.
Her (later): OK, I finished early. I can meet you. :)

Notice how the only bit of "game" I threw at her was when she showed hesitance to meet up. The only reason I did this is because I knew I was going to lose her if I didn't amp things up, show my desire for her again and polarize things a bit to prevent the flake. I did that. And it worked.

Or did it?

Natalie never showed up. She called me at about 7:40 PM and explained to me that although she liked me a lot that because I was leaving England in a few days she couldn't justify coming on a date with me. It was clear she felt bad about it, but her values were clear.

I respected that decision and told her that it was fine, that she was a beautiful girl, and that she deserves a great guy who will stick around. And I meant it.

And unfortunately, this has consistently been my experience. A flake is a flake. No matter what you do. Even if you can create a temporary illusion that she wants to meet up with you.

If anything, being cute and trying to impress her will only hurt you, as it will come across as needy and unattractive. One of the quickest ways to lose a girl is by texting her stuff that's way too try-hard.

When in doubt, be plain and to-the-point.

This often disappoints some guys. They get really excited about sending fancy or brilliant texts that magically change a girl's mind on a dime. Don't bother. Short of lying or manipulation, it almost never works.

You're not going to be texting Shakespearean Sonnets to her. Get her to agree to meet up as soon as possible and then do all of the heavy lifting in person, where you can interact physically, where she can see your intentions and your non-neediness, and where you're not limited to 120 characters at a time or whatever.

The Perfect Date

Despite how nervous you get beforehand, dates are perhaps the most straightforward part of this entire process. Go to the right venues, go at the right times, avoid the obvious pitfalls, and you should be in the clear.

<u>When to Go on Dates:</u> Don't do lunch dates, and never make an afternoon date the first date if possible. Just don't do it. For whatever reason, nothing says, "let's just be friends" more than having lunch together.

Save dates for the nighttime. It builds a greater sense of expectation. There's more flexibility to spend more time together. It's more of a commitment. And neither of you are in a rush to be anywhere in an hour. It also leaves the option open for you or her sleeping over.

As far as when to go, it's going to depend a lot on what you're doing. But you want to allow yourself time for at least three one-hour activities (more on that later). So anywhere between 6 PM to 9 PM. Later than that, and you limit your time together. Earlier than that, and you get a daytime vibe and the date will usually run out of steam before she has to go home. You want to time the date so that you are peaking together at around 10 PM or 11 PM and she has the, "I need to go home, but I don't want to yet," feeling.

<u>Where to Go:</u> Absolutely no movie dates for first or second dates. Movie dates are terrible. You don't get to talk, you sit awkwardly next to each other, and it's impossible to touch her without being awkward (importance of this in the next chapter).

Avoid dinner dates if at all possible. They're cliché. They can be somewhat impersonal depending on where you eat. Once again, it's almost impossible to touch. And believe it or not, a lot of women are self-conscious about eating in front of you, food selection, etc. Also, you can avoid the awkward "who pays?" situation — which we'll talk about in the next section.

Good date locations are locations that are active, participatory, and allow for touching and flirting. Alcohol can be helpful as well if that's your style. Some good examples include comedy clubs, dance classes, museum exhibits, walks in interesting places (plazas, parks, etc.), concerts, or just grabbing a drink somewhere.

A lot of places to go will depend on your town. I recommend using Yelp.com to find interesting places around you. For instance, there used to be a bowling alley/nightclub venue near my old apartment in Boston. It was a lot of fun. You could bowl together (participatory, active, allows flirting) as well as have a few drinks, and if things went well and we were in a party mood, we could go downstairs and dance.

Bars and nightclubs are fine if you both are into those kinds of venues. Just make sure that if you go, you end up there alone. A date with friends is not a date. This will often happen if she suggests a bar to go — "Oh, we can meet my friend Cindy there…" Chances are if she wants to hang out with her friend with you, then it's no longer a date.

Finally, you should find venues and activities that are close to either your place or her place. What I recommend doing is researching and finding at least 4-6 good date venues or activities that are within a short drive of your house or apartment. Even better is if you can find a few places that are within walking distance.

The logic is simple: the closer the venues are to your place or hers, the less travel time necessary, the fewer logistical headaches, and the better the chance of you ending up at each other's houses at the end of the night.

Once you've researched and found 4-6 venues and activities near your place that you enjoy doing, that are good date activities and are easily accessible, it's time to start putting them together and do multiple things on each date.

This may sound weird to you, but this is key. Most men do dinner and then sit at the table for another hour chatting away. There's little flirting. No activity. No touching. No sense of dynamics or change.

On our dates, we are *doing* things — lots of things. We're going bowling, having drinks, dancing, checking out statues in the park and carriage riding — all in three hours.

There's something strange in human psychology. Our level of intimacy with one another doesn't just come from how much we talk about as much as it comes from the experiences we share. These dates are designed to create as much mutual experience as possible in the least amount of time possible. Here are some examples of solid dates:

Meet for coffee → get ice cream down the street → check out the big swing in the park → shopping together at quirky bookstore

Salsa class → drinks next door afterward → walk to neighborhood pizza place → video games at your place

Window shopping at local shopping center → improv comedy show → quick dinner afterward → walk around local park

Include dancing if at all possible, as it's the most sexual date activity you can have. Also, if you two decide to drink, try to drink at the second or last venues/activities. You don't ever want to end up hammered on a date.

<u>How to Behave on a Date</u>: As I mentioned before, you want your dates to be interactive. You want to be able to walk around, be able to touch and be as interactive as possible.

The underlying concept to have on a date is that you should try to constantly be leading.

Every decision should be yours and she should be expected to follow it. Remove, "What do you want to do now?" from your dating vocabulary. Never say it again.

It should be like this: "Hey, let's grab some tacos, I know a cool stand over here," "I got an idea, I'm going to kick your ass in air hockey," "Let's check out the Science museum, they have an awesome exhibit on the human body," etc.

As far as what to talk about, your conversations should be getting deeper and more personal. There should be less teasing and playful banter and more conversations about your lives and what's important to you. Learn about her past, her passions, her dreams, what her favorite things are.

At the same time, you don't want to turn this into a job interview (which too many dinner dates turn into), but elicit these topics by sharing them yourself.

Finally, the big question in our post-feminism world: who pays? These days, most women will offer to pay out of politeness, but you're supposed to turn them down because it's the gentleman thing to do (or something like that). Look, I didn't make this stuff up, but after being on probably

100+ dates with dozens of women, and getting into more than a few awkward situations about paying, this is what works for me: pay unless she physically pulls out her wallet/credit card and stops you. Until she physically does that, just pay.

Yes, once in a while you can get women buying you drinks and stuff — there are even ways to influence them to do this — but at the end of the day, unless you're broke, take care of them. It's a no-lose move and it will win you points with many of them.

Chapter 14
Physicality and Sex

Let's talk about sex. And more specifically, why women have it, and why they would ever want to have it with you.

Female sexuality has been a murky area in psychology for almost a century now. Freud famously said at one point, "The great question that has never been answered, and which I have not yet been able to answer, despite my thirty years of research into the feminine soul, is 'what do women want?'"

Among researchers, it was long thought that female arousal was tied to ideas and display of security, investment and commitment, particularly from high-status men.

But if you think about it, you know, here in the real world, this doesn't really make sense. Because unfortunately for psychologists, women don't light candles and lay in their bathtubs masturbating to a mortgage and a white picket fence. They fantasize about far different (and stranger) things.

In her book, *My Secret Garden*, the journalist Nancy Friday collected anonymous sexual fantasies from women around the world. If you ever want your mind expanded in an interesting way, check it out. There are women out there who get turned on by some really, well, let's call it "creative" stuff. We're talking about gangbangs, rape, weird locations and positions, anonymous men, and so on and so forth.

So this sort of data threw a bit of a monkey wrench into everything. For many years, scientists didn't really know where to start. With men it was pretty easy — we're primarily visually stimulated, and we generally all like similar features (symmetry, certain hip/waist ratio, large breasts, etc.)

But with women, you may as well throw shit at a dartboard because that's about as far as things were getting.

One new conclusion in arousal research these days is that female arousal is somewhat narcissistic in nature. Women are turned on by being wanted, by being desired.

(Note: Men are as well, although since female arousal is affected more by psychological stimuli than physical stimuli on average, this is far more important for female arousal.)

This actually explains some the odd and disparate things that seem to turn some women on. Seemingly disconnected events that arouse women — a romantic marriage proposal in one instance, being tied up to the bathroom sink in another — make sense when viewed this way. Both indicate an extreme desire in her by a man. A man who's willing to sacrifice everything to be with her. In one instance, the man is willing to commit his entire life to her. In another he's, willing to go to physical extremes for her. Both are hot.

When women say that just because they have rape fantasies doesn't mean they want to be raped, this is what they mean. What they want is to be desired. An unhinged desire. A passionate and uncontrollable desire. They want to be desired to the point that a man completely loses awareness and self-control. The actual rape part — I'm sure none of them would actually enjoy.

My experience supports this as well. Those in the men's dating advice industry have discovered over the past five years or so that the more assertively you pursue a woman, the more aroused she becomes. There's something almost "magical" about an uninhibited physicality when being with a woman.

Something as simple as taking a guy who usually stands there blabbering for hours about meteorology or something, if you take that same guy and have him put his arm around the woman he's talking to or have him lightly touch her as if punctuating his points and jokes, this generates way more sexual tension.

Indeed, sexuality, in the end, is all about movement and our bodies entwining themselves. Everything else is kind of just a means to reach that point.

I'm going to say this point-blank: getting physical with women, and getting physical quickly and comfortably, is ultimately the difference between having a lot of female friends, and having a lot of girlfriends and dates.

Being physical with women is by far the most integral piece of seduction and dating women. If you have it, you will constantly have options. If you don't, you will spend a lot of time alone.

I have a friend. He's a decent-looking guy. He almost never approaches (except when he's drunk). He's awkward to talk to. He has a strange sense of humor. But he gets physical with women. He touches them early. He touches them often. And even if they don't reciprocate or move away. He tries again. In other words, he's always going for it.

And you know what? He gets laid constantly. With hot women too.

It's amazing. I used to hang out with him and would watch him awkwardly stumble around conversations, drink a little too much, and awkwardly putting his arm around girls as the girls sat there with a look of confusion. I'd watch him and think to myself, "Oh man, what a disaster."

And then I'd come back 20 minutes later and he'd be making out with her. And then an hour later she'd be excitedly going home with him.

He just has no inhibitions whatsoever about going for it. Unless the girl would clearly stop him or say "No!" he would always be going for it. And the women loved it. They loved his physicality and his raw sexual energy. It made them feel beautiful and sexy and it was exciting.

(Ethical note here: if a woman clearly tells you to stop doing something, stop. Don't take offense, but instead, ask her if she's uncomfortable and/or why she's uncomfortable. Often it's not that she doesn't like you, it's just that you're moving too fast for her. Always respect her boundaries and clarify as early as possible what she's comfortable with and what her expectations are. Not only is this the vulnerable thing to do, it's also the respectful thing to do.)

Being physical with women is a necessary habit that most men who are poor with women never do. Most men are a bit shy and hesitant when it comes to "making moves:" touching, the first kiss, sexual touching, etc. Well, that needs to stop. From now on, you are a sexually assertive and dominant guy and you have no shame about it. We'll also discover that women actually prefer you to be this way.

215

There are two reasons for being physically assertive with women. The first is polarization. You want to establish whether she's sexually interested in you as soon as you possibly can. The second reason is that being physical is bold and, therefore, a highly attractive form of flirting.

Studies have shown that people being touched by somebody when they first meet them not only have a much higher probability of thinking favorably of them, but they also were shown to trust them quicker.

So how do you touch a girl right off the bat?

As you having a conversation with her, assuming she is Receptive, just lightly touch her on the arm, near the elbow. Don't press hard or hold it, as that could startle her, but just a small brush or tap or light squeeze. Use your touching to punctuate the conversation, as if emphasizing a funny moment or the punchline of the joke. Think of touching as the exclamation marks or question marks of the dialogue.

For instance, let's say you make a clever joke and she begins to laugh really hard, you should put your hand on her arm to punctuate the emotion of the moment.

The best way to touch is to integrate physicality into your conversation. For example, using games such as thumb wars, twirling her like a ballerina, or giving high fives are great ways to initiate physical contact. As the conversation goes on, the better things are going, the more you want to be touching and the more personal you want your touches to be.

Your touching should happen in a progression. In general, you want to start on the outside of her body — her arms and legs — and slowly move closer into her body. Put your hand on her back as you move her to sit down with you, put your arm around her lower back as she leans against the bar next to you, etc. Later on, this progression will continue into intimacy: tickling, massages, and cuddling (or spooning). And from there it will continue on into kissing, petting, and becoming sexual.

Signals Women Give

Men are notoriously bad at recognizing "signals" women give them when they're interested. In the courtship process, it's always the man's responsibility to take action and make the moves, and the woman's responsibility to give him signals, telling him when to proceed and when to stop.

Throughout this chapter, we will be discussing physically escalating with a woman. This involves touching her in sexual ways.

As men, we're kind of stuck in a weird place. Because on the one hand, we're always expected to initiate and make the first move. But on the other, we're supposed to respect a woman's desires and right to her own body.

This is why before proceeding with advice about getting sexual with women, I want to take a moment to list out the signals women give that indicate she is sexually interested in you. You should see these somewhat as invitations to proceed with them physically, although due to potential miscommunication, don't make too many assumptions. What we're looking for is a consistent stream of signals coming from her to you. Pre-approach signals mean she wants to talk to you. Conversational signals mean she wants to get closer to you physically. And escalation signals mean that she wants to get sexual with you.

View these signals as green lights when they come up, but only to move to the next group of signals (i.e., just because a woman makes eye contact with you doesn't mean she wants to fuck you right then and there, it just means she's curious about talking to you.) Take it one step at a time, and remember, she always has the right to back out or change her mind at any moment.

Pre-Approach Signals

- Non-Accidental Eye Contact: When in doubt, assume it's not accidental. Humans are programmed to look at and focus on whatever they're either curious about or what they find attractive. If she's looking at you even 10% more than the average stranger, then she's at least somewhat curious/interested in you. I make a point to approach every woman who makes non-accidental eye contact with me, and it serves me well.

- Smiling: If eye contact means she's interested, this means "you better come talk to me!"

- She Approaches You: This goes without saying, although a lot of guys are so oblivious, they even miss this. If a woman approaches you, even if it's to ask the time, about the weather, for directions, or whatever, chances are she has some interest in talking to you.

217

- Proximity: This one is subtle, but the more you work on your lifestyle, body language, and style, the more of these you will get. It's when a woman places herself conspicuously near you when she doesn't have to. For instance, let's say you're sitting on a bus and an attractive woman gets on. The entire bus is empty, yet she comes over and sits across from you. This could mean she wants you to talk to her. Some other examples are when a woman comes and stands near you in a store or shop looking at nothing in particular for a long amount of time.

Conversation Signals

- Excessive Smiling/Laughing: This is subjective and will require some judgment, but sometimes you will notice one girl smiling and laughing a lot more than others when you speak. Chances are she likes you.

- Flipping or Playing with Her Hair: Classic signal of flirtation and often done unconsciously.

- Eyes Dilate: Studies have shown our eyes dilate when we look at someone we're attracted to. Hard to notice, especially in some nighttime scenario. But this gives her eyes a much bigger and wider look than normal, what you may call "big doe eyes."

- Standing Closer to You Than Normal: self-explanatory. Pay attention to where she positions herself while talking to you. If it's slightly within your bubble of personal space that probably indicates she's interested in getting physical with you.

- Excessive Eye Contact: Same as excessive smiling. If she's locked onto your gaze during a conversation, that means she's very interested in what you have to say. Most people break eye contact very often, especially with people they just met. If she doesn't, that means she's interested in you.

- Prioritizes You: Another very subjective one. This can be very subtle. But it's when her actions subtly show you that she prioritizes you over interacting with others. The classic example here is if you meet a girl at a bar and her friends come over and try to talk to her and she ignores her friends. Most women, if they don't like you, will drop you like a hot potato when their friends come around. But if she ignores her friends or stays with you, that's a clear indication that she likes you.

<u>Escalation Signals</u>

- Isolates Herself with You: Oftentimes the most overt advances a woman will make won't be in actually making a move (that's your job), but they'll actively work to put you in the easiest situation possible. Let's say I've been hanging out with a woman at a small party for most of the night and she suddenly she says, "let's take a walk around the block, it's noisy in here," she's purposely isolating herself with me as much as possible. This typically means she wants to be kissed.

- Ditches Her Friends For You: Goes along with the above; it takes a lot for a woman to leave her friends behind for a guy, especially one she's only known for a few hours or one night. If she does this, take it as a bright green light.

- Touches You: If she starts putting her hands on your arms or legs or is demonstrating (or reciprocating) any of the touching I described in the previous section, this is a clear signal: she is sexually interested in you and wants to be kissed.

When To Go For the Kiss

When it comes to kissing a woman, there's an old adage amongst dating coaches: if you think you can kiss her, you probably could have ten minutes ago. We men are horrible at gauging a woman's sexual desire and when she's ready to move things forward.

So, in general, it's safe to assume that anytime you think you could kiss her, you probably already could have. Too many guys get hung up looking for "sign" after "sign" when women have been giving them signals all night. Think of it this way: it's much better to try and kiss her and get rejected than to go the whole night without making a move and never knowing what would have been.

So the rule of thumb is, when in doubt, go for it.

If you go in for the kiss and she turns her head or doesn't reciprocate, pull back and ask her how she's feeling, if she likes you or if you're moving too fast. Listen to her response, often women will want to kiss you but

219

there's something that's worrying them or upsetting them or making them self-conscious. The best way to deal with this is through vulnerability and simply asking her to be honest with whatever the issue is.

There are some women who don't kiss in public places. They feel like it's in bad taste and poor form. No matter how much they like you, they won't do it.

The same goes if she's in front of a bunch of people she knows. If she's standing right next to four of her co-workers, she's probably not going to feel comfortable making out with you. Try moving her somewhere more private.

Some notes on kissing well:

- *Don't* slobber all over her face.
- *Don't* jam your tongue down her throat. Heavy tongue has its place, but it's usually in the bedroom when you guys are naked.
- *Don't* peck her like she's your grandmother.
- *Don't* shove your face into hers or apply too much pressure. Kisses are sensual. Imagine you're massaging her lips with yours.

A lot of kissing revolves around how you use your hands as well. Your hands should be roaming her body gently, caressing her back, gently holding her neck, pulling her hips into yours. One of my favorite things to do while making out with a girl is to grab her belt loops on her pants and pull her hips into mine.

Don't get ahead of yourself when you're kissing. Too many men start making out with a woman and then immediately go into "OK, LET'S FUCK" mode where they practically start molesting her wherever they are and devouring her face.

Cool it. Kissing is simply the gateway to greater and deeper intimacy. Enjoy it, play with it, relax into it.

Moving Forward and Consent

So you've kissed her. Now what?

Assuming you're in a discrete place, you've both gotten to know each other, and you're both "fuck yes" about going further, then it's time to escalate things towards sex.

220

Usually, the place to touch a woman that indicates you're ready for sex and that isn't acceptable unless she is as well are her breasts. If your hands find your way to them and she's into it, then this is usually an indication that things are going to go further.

But believe it or not, women don't just want to drop their pants and screw right there on the spot. Whereas men are like a microwave that you just press a button and the food is ready to go, women are like an oven. They need to be warmed up, pre-heated even. Remember, female arousal is primarily psychological. Therefore, there needs to be a sense of build-up to sex. You don't just go from kissing to screwing (some women do, but typically not). Usually, you need to build up from light touching, to kissing, to kissing plus roaming hands, to some clothes off and more touching, and so on.

Women will often object at this point and say they just want to mess around and not have sex itself. The correct answer to any objection is always, "That's fine. We'll do whatever you're comfortable doing." The point is to have an enjoyable experience, not to get more notches on your bedpost.

Yes, women often say, "We're not going to have sex tonight," and then go ahead and have sex. And that's fine too. Just accept that these things are often fluid and both you and her can opt in or opt out at any time without shame or judgment.

A quick note about rape because unfortunately I have to put something in here: remember, our general guideline here is that we continue until a woman makes us stop. This means she physically stops you — i.e., moves your hands off of her, moves away from you, puts her clothes back on, etc. — or clearly and verbally says, "STOP!" or "NO!"

If she's incapacitated to the point (drunk, drugs, etc.) where she probably couldn't opt out or make a clear decision, then you should stop. End of story.

Physicality is something you have to practice and become comfortable at. Every man develops his own style and personality to how he likes to touch, where he likes to touch, how he likes to move things forward. And as you develop your own style of physicality, you will begin to get a sense for when women are comfortable with what. The important thing is to see sex as not something you are earning or taking from a woman, but rather something you two are participating in together. It's a team effort.

221

Because, believe it or not, women want sex too. They want wild, passionate, crazy sex, just like you do.

Sex

Oh my God bro, you're totally going to get laid tonight!

No, seriously. Once you've got some clothes off and you're both on a bed, a couch, the bathroom floor — or wherever you plan on doing the dirty — you've now entered the realm of foreplay. Sadly, men overlook foreplay because we're just too damn excited about getting our dicks wet. The more foreplay there is, the hotter your woman's going to be, the better sex she's going to have, which means the better sex you'll have (this is a team sport, remember?)

A good place to start is by sucking and massaging her bare breasts. Some girls who like it rougher like it when you gently bite on their nipples, but be careful, not every girl is into that.

From there, you should at least finger her or rub her clitoris. Feel how wet she is. If she's wet, then slowly keep moving things forward. If she's dry then slow down and take your time. She needs more time to get warmed up.

If you enjoy giving girls oral sex, this is an excellent time to do that as well. If you give good oral sex, most girls won't be able to resist the urge to have sex then and there (some will even grab you and make you do it).

The most important thing to keep in mind about foreplay is the concept of teasing or expectation. As you do the things talked about above, don't just rush into them and devour her. That can be cool sometimes, but in general, you want to take things slow, create a drawn-out and sensual experience. Girls love to be teased. For instance, instead of just shoving your finger inside her and going at it, trying lightly touching her pussy with your fingertips for a few seconds. She'll go crazy and want you inside her more than ever.

Instead of just giving her oral sex, start off slow by kissing the inside of her thighs, inching closer and closer. Create expectation. Make her yearn for whatever you're about to do to her. Stuff like this drives girls crazy and makes them incredibly horny. If you do this well and repeatedly, you'll often get girls pushing *you* down and forcing *you* to have sex. The expectation is too much. They have to have it. Right then and there.

When it comes to sex, more important than any physical technique — some cool angle or position or whatever — is being dominant. Sexual gratification for women is far more psychological than it is physical, whereas for men it's mostly physical. A large component of this psychological satisfaction comes from being dominated and surrendering control. Women like to feel like you have the power and the control in the bedroom. They want you to be assertive and strong with what you want. So how do you become dominant in bed?

1. Be loud. Make noise. Grunt. Breathe hard. Women love this because it makes them feel like they can be loud. And when they're loud they get off easier and more often.

2. Talk dirty. Tell her how sexy she is. Tell her what you're going to do to her before you do it. Call her a dirty girl and a horny slut. This may be outside of your comfort zone, but realize that in the bedroom the rules change and logic goes out the window.

3. Get physical. Spank her. Pull her hair. Hold her down with one hand. When you change positions, literally pick her up and move her yourself.

4. Don't ever ask, "Is this OK? Do you want to do X?" Just do it and stop later if she doesn't like it and apologize. Nothing turns a girl off faster than a guy who defers to her too much while having sex. Take control. Do what turns you on and that will then turn her on.

The most important habit to develop, by far, is to talk and be expressive in the bedroom. There has to be an open forum of communication when you sleep with a woman, especially the first few times you're together. Sex is always somewhat awkward the first time you're with a new person. Everybody engages in different practices, habits and prefers different things. It takes a while to learn each other's tendencies and adapt to one another's likes and dislikes.

This requires you to have a sense of humor in the bedroom. Goofy and weird moments are going to happen in the sack and most people are at their most insecure when they're naked and lying under someone they just met a week ago.

Have a sense of humor. Be understanding. *Relax*.

One of my favorite jokes in the bedroom, when stuff goes awry, is, "They make it look so easy in the movies." If you can get a girl to crack up, she'll forget she's naked, forget she's in a strange position and forget that you just screwed up and just be with you, laughing with you.

Also, be honest. If you don't like the way she gives a blowjob, tell her and then tell her how you do like it. But also, be honest with the compliments. Tell her she's beautiful naked. Tell her you love how she rides you. Tell her she looks sexy in that position.

Be open and honest. Communicate. The most important factor for good sex is how comfortable the two people are around each other. (This is another argument for practicing vulnerability, by the way.)

A lot of men feel anxious around sexuality and actually get nervous once they know they're going to have it. But if you bring up sexual anxiety, almost every guy will laugh and say, "Must suck for that guy," as if they don't have any. The rotten truth is that most of us have some form of it or another. There are a variety of causes for sexual anxiety, but the most common are:

- Inexperience
- Strict religious and/or cultural upbringing
- Negative past sexual experiences
- Past emotional trauma
- Low self-esteem

Ultimately, the causes of sexual anxiety are directly related to other forms of anxiety: lack of confidence, high investment in others, shame, and a fear of vulnerability.

There are two symptoms, and you either have one or the other. You either cum way too fast (less than a minute or two) or you either can't get hard or you can't keep it hard.

But that doesn't make sense. How can two completely opposite phenomena be caused by the same thing?

It's basically a permutation of the "fight or flight" response. The idea is that when you become nervous and adrenaline is released, your body wants to get itself into a protected and safe position as soon as possible. One way to do this is to ejaculate immediately. The other is to lose your erection entirely.

Either way, these problems suck. I'm not sure which one's worse. But we have ways to combat this problem.

If you finish way too quickly, try finding a thicker condom. They actually make condoms now that purposely numb your penis so that you can last longer. Try masturbating a few hours before you expect to have sex.

If you have trouble getting it up or keeping it up, get pills. Seriously, there are herbal supplements that you can buy over the counter that act similarly to Viagra. They make you hard as an ox and able to go multiple times. Take a couple before you get intimate with a girl and you shouldn't have any problems keeping it at attention.

But these remedies are merely Band-Aid solutions for a larger problem.

The larger problem is not being completely comfortable with your sexuality and having sex. It's once again a vulnerability issue. This problem reaches much deeper and lurks within our subconscious. The most obvious solution is to simply have as much sex as possible. Getting a steady girlfriend is the best way to do this.

Unfortunately, if you want to stay single, this will take a lot of time and effort. And you have to deal with a lot of demoralizing failures. Try taking it slow with the girl once you know you're going to have sex with her.

Think of it as having to make *yourself* more secure and comfortable around her until you're able to have sex. I know it sounds lame, but it's true. Slow things down, enjoy the foreplay more, and don't pressure yourself to get to it until you're good and ready.

Practice closing your eyes and relaxing when you know you'll be having sex with her. If you have trouble with getting too excited, think about something non-sexual like baseball or video games. If you have trouble getting it up, relax and just look at her and think about how sexy she is.

If you feel that you have some sort of emotional trauma in your past or were raised in a seriously sexually repressed environment, consider seeking counseling or therapy.

Regardless, once you've reached this point, you've reached the point of maximum vulnerability with one person. Typically, women become more invested after sex and men become less invested after sex. The power dynamic in most couples will switch at this point. The power of choice that the woman had (whether to have sex or not) now usually switches over to the man (whether to commit or not). If this power dynamic doesn't switch, it's usually a sign of neediness in the man, and the attraction will not last.

Vulnerability need not be confused with commitment or attachment. It's still possible to experience an intense and powerful emotional connection with a woman and never desire long-term commitment with one another.

But at the same time, this sort of vulnerability and intimacy is often the starting point of an attachment within most of us that will never go away. To this day, women I have slept with exist within a separate category of friendship and loyalty in my mind, even if I didn't end up dating them.

While intimacy, romance, and intense emotional connection are fantastic and in many ways intoxicating, like a drug and even possibly addictive, true, long-lasting emotional connection can only come through submitting to long-term commitment. But that is a topic for another book.

Closing

Conclusion:
Moving Ahead

There's a lot to digest in this book. And if you're a first-timer who hasn't started his journey of self-improvement to become more attractive to women, it's easy to get overwhelmed and wonder where to start.

That's why I've put together this small Action Plan at the end of the book, to not only give you a clear place to start but also help you see what you should focus on and in which order.

The Action Plan is divided up into sections of five tasks or challenges. Once you've completed at least four of the tasks in each section, move on to the next section. In Section 1, some tasks you will naturally have handled. For instance, if you already work out regularly, then that's fine. In other sections, an item doesn't count unless you do it *since starting that section*. For instance, in Section 5, you're challenged to have sex with a woman you've never had sex with before. Obviously, not everyone reading this is a virgin. Some of you may even have sex with a woman in previous sections. But it doesn't count until you get to section 5.

Obviously, these aren't rigid rules. But the sections are laid out here to challenge you and give you clearly defined goals and benchmarks to strive for. In all sections, some tasks will be very easy for you. Others will be very difficult. It will vary from person to person, but the idea is to give you a general path to follow when it comes to improving yourself.

Also realize, that this is a long-term process. A lot of these tasks won't be completed in one night or even in one weekend. A lot of them will require weeks or months of effort. But that's OK. That means you probably really needed to work on it.

Level 1: Your Foundation (Complete 5 of 5)

Join a gym: If you're not already a member of a gym, join one. If you're not familiar with how to work out properly, hire a personal trainer. Make this a weekly habit.

Upgrade your wardrobe: Go out and upgrade your wardrobe based on the recommendations in Chapter 8. Challenge yourself to wear nicer clothes than you've ever worn before. It'll change how you feel about yourself.

Get a nice haircut: Go to a salon and drop the $50 on it. It's worth it. It makes a difference.

Job security/satisfaction: This is a complicated one, but if you're not happy with your work situation, take some time and plan a way to fix it. If you work too much, try to find a way to work less. If you're unemployed, stop everything else and get a job.

Pursue one social hobby regularly: Pick a social hobby and pursue it regularly. You may already have one, but if not, find one. It could be dance classes, public speaking courses, language courses, cooking classes, joining a band, etc. Whatever it is, make it social. That means sitting at home and perfecting your model airplanes doesn't count.

Level 2: Meeting Women (Complete 4 of 5)

Figure out demographics: Figure out your demographics based on the recommendations in. Write down the type of women you'd like to meet and the places you enjoy going most. Then find venues or events where those two things intersect. It could be independent rock concerts, it could be art gallery showings, it could be salsa nights. Whatever it is, find your niche and pursue it.

Meet 5 women in one day: Self-explanatory

Meet 20 women in one week: Also self-explanatory.

Join an online dating site and email 10 women: Also self-explanatory. If you're under 30 years old, I recommend free dating sites. If you're over 30 years old, I recommend pay sites.

Sign up for a singles or speed dating event: If you have trouble doing the approaching tasks, then this may give you a needed boost in the right direction.

Level 3: Getting to Know Women (Complete 2 of 3)

Hold at least three 30-minute conversations with women you just met: Can be anywhere.

Get three phone numbers from women you just met: Just ask, you'll be surprised how many women will give them to you.

Go on two dates: They can come from women you met anywhere.

Level 4: Getting Intimate (Complete 2 of 3)

Kiss two women: Make sure they're women you've met since reading this book.

Go on a second date with the same woman: Self-explanatory.

Successfully get a woman back to your place: Usually can be done on the second date.

Level 5: Getting Sexual (Complete 2 of 2)

Have sex with a woman you've never had sex with before: Self explanatory

Go on three first dates with new women: Self-explanatory.

Level 6: Oh, You Mack Daddy, You (Optional)

Have sex with a woman you met that same day/night: Again, recommended you do this with a woman you meet in a bar or nightclub. Bringing a woman home you meet during the day is more difficult, but not impossible.

Have sex with a woman on the first date: Make sure it's a damn good date.

Kiss three women the day/night you meet them: Can be done on separate nights. Also recommended to do this at a bar or nightclub.

Epilogue:
What If It Was a Gift?

Over the course of the previous 230 pages, we've discovered that attraction flows from women perceiving non-neediness and a sense of inner security in men. This confidence and security arise from having a stronger identity and investment in oneself than in the perception of others. This sub-communicates that as a man, you're dependable, confident and high status (or likely to become high status).

The way to cultivate a higher investment in oneself, the way to becoming more confident, is actually counterintuitive. We learned that showing vulnerability, both in emotion and action, actually leads to a higher investment in oneself and higher non-neediness.

This newfound confidence then allows you to express yourself more clearly and directly. When you express yourself more clearly and directly, you polarize the reactions of women, opening yourself up to more rejection, but also attracting other women stronger than ever before. Attracting women occurs through a process of self-selection. The rate at which you attract them happens through a process of overcoming fear. And the consistency in which you seduce those women attracted happens through a process of expressing your sexuality. These are the three fundamentals.

Presented in these pages are all of the tools I can ever imagine a man ever needing to renovate himself and become more successful with women. Undoubtedly for you, it will be difficult at times. You will run into speed bumps, detours, distractions, and emotional highs lows. But if you persist and stay optimistic, you will get there. I'm absolutely sure of it.

And in those times that it does become difficult, those times where you do get frustrated and fall back to your unconfident beliefs, your desire for external validation, where you let yourself become swayed by the whims of others rather than your internal compass, you may feel lost or hopeless. This feeling of hopelessness may last for minutes, hours or days, but chances are if you push yourself, if you genuinely try to change yourself and re-orient how you interact with the world, then you will feel it at some point.

And for those times, let me share with you a phrase that has helped me and countless other men through those dire straits.

The phrase comes from Dr. Robert Glover and his book *No More Mr. Nice Guy*, one of the best books I've ever read on men's emotional health and development.

The phrase is: "What if it was a gift?"

Whatever happens to you, no matter how bad, no matter how bleak you feel, ask yourself, "What if it was a gift?" and then try to rationalize a way it could be so.

Because you see, in the world of emotions, there are no absolutes; you can usually draw whichever conclusions you desire. So why not choose to draw conclusions of blessings, positivity, and gifts?

Ex-girlfriend dumps you and left you for another man. What if it was a gift? Because without her, you would not have been put on this path of self-improvement, and you would have forever been stuck in a relationship full of deceit and without self-awareness.

A woman makes fun of your hair and calls you ugly. What if it was a gift? Such a harsh rejection will steel you into becoming even more confident in the future, and hopefully, will inspire you to re-evaluate how you look.

Your friends tell you that approaching women is creepy and that you're a loser for wanting to do it. What if it was a gift? It shows that what you're doing and what you're working on is pushing social boundaries, is polarizing, and is ultimately making you more controversial and attractive.

When I was 19 years old, a friend of mine drowned right in front of me. We were at a party on a lake. One minute he was there, laughing, smiling, joking, and the next moment he was gone. Forever.

It was one of the biggest gifts I've ever been given. Not because it was good. It was tragic. But because of how it affected me ever since.

Obviously, that night was shocking and traumatizing. But I came away from the experience with a keen awareness of how transient this existence is. How any of us can be taken at any moment. How no one is going to live my life for me, and every second I spend sitting around feeling distant from my true desires, avoiding the world and being afraid to engage it, is a second that I'm forfeiting the biggest gift of all: my time here in this life.

His death shocked me, depressed me and scared me, but it scared me into having the courage to take risks, to express myself, to invest in my self-perception more than the perceptions of others. Because after all, sooner or later this will all disappear, and none of it will matter. So you might as well make the most of it while you're here.

And ultimately, that's all that I can hope for you. That you make the most of your time here. That you take the tools I've laid out here and go out and forge a unique path for yourself and experience the love, the thrills, and the happiness that this life can reward you.

Because that is what life does: it rewards you. It's giving you gifts every day.

Are you going to accept them?

Glossary

Anxiety — A general emotional state of fear and apprehension brought on repeatedly by a certain situation. Anxiety is conquered through Courage. *See Also: Sexual Anxiety, Social Anxiety, Courage*

Arousal — The process in which someone is sexually stimulated, physically, psychologically or emotionally. Current research posits women are primarily aroused through displays of sexual intent and bold behaviors. *See Also: Sexual Intent, Courage*

Assortment Effect — The psychological term for the observed tendency for men and women of similar beliefs and self-perceptions to attract one another. For instance, a man with low self-esteem will attract women with low self-esteem. A man with a positive attitude towards sex will attract women with positive attitudes towards sex. *See Also: Demographics*

Attractive Behavior — Confident behavior, both in one's everyday life, as well as direct interactions with women. Attractive behavior is usually a result of vulnerability, although not always. *See Also: Lifestyle, Neediness*

Boundaries — The limit of interaction and communication one finds acceptable. Boundaries can be strong or weak based upon the person's confidence level. For instance, John lacks confidence and therefore lets his dates make fun of him without saying anything. Sally has high confidence and does not tolerate her date being 20 minutes late to pick her up. Strong boundaries are both a cause and effect of True Confidence. Standing up for one's boundaries often triggers attraction and always generates greater respect. *See Also: True Confidence*

Confidence — One's belief in themselves and their ability and competence in a certain situation. Confidence is context-dependent. One can be confident in a boardroom but horribly unconfident in a sexual relationship. Confidence is often confused with self-esteem. Lack of confidence in romantic situations is a reflection of neediness, which is a component of low self-esteem. Confident behavior is always attractive. *See Also: Non-Neediness, Neediness, Self-Esteem*

Courage — The ability to perform an action despite feeling fear and anxiety about doing it. *See Also: Anxiety*

Creepy — To express one's sexuality in such a way that makes a woman uncomfortable or less secure. Creepy behavior can happen consciously or unconsciously. *See Also: Sexual Intent, Flirting*

Dating Success — Maximizing one's happiness with the woman/women one chooses. It is important to note that it is NOT determined by numbers, sexual encounters, appearances, etc., but by happiness.

Defense Mechanisms — Psychological reactions to anxiety that cause one to avoid taking action. Examples include blame, anger, projection, rationalizations, apathy, etc. *See Also: Anxiety, Courage*

Demographics — The idea that you will experience greater success (happiness) and efficiency by pursuing women in areas of your life that you excel at or enjoy. For instance, if you are a musician, then you are more likely to experience dating success by meeting women at concerts and music events. *See Also: Assortment Effect, Lifestyle*

Emotional Connection — A mutual emotional investment between two people. This investment generates a feeling of closeness and greater empathy. Can often trigger arousal and sexual desire.

Finding Your Truth — A two-part process of 1) removing behaviors which are based on receiving the approval of others rather than your own values and 2) getting in touch with emotions and desires which were previously unconscious. Finding one's truth is based on the idea that most of our behaviors and beliefs are actually unconscious habits we picked up for the wrong reasons throughout our lives. Getting in touch with one's real emotions and desires and discarding the unconfident habits and behaviors leads one to become more vulnerable, more confident, and, therefore, more attractive. *See Also: Attractive Behavior, Non-Neediness, Vulnerability*

Flake — A specific form of rejection. When a woman demonstrates interest or says she will see you again and then never does.

Flirting — The demonstration of sexual intent in a fun and playful manner. Successful flirting makes women feel secure with your sexual intent. The opposite of creepy. *See Also: Creepy, Sexual Intent*

Friction — Circumstances and causes that prevent sexual escalation from occurring despite there being mutual attraction. For instance, two people may be very attracted to one another, but one is married and the other lives in another town.

Honest Action — Removing the separation between what one desires to do and what one actually does. Usually involves overcoming one's own anxieties and limiting beliefs about what is possible.

Honest Communication — Removing the separation between what one believes and feels and what one says. Requires a removal of inhibitions as well as a clarity to one's communication.

Honest Living — Removing the separation between the person you desire to be and the person you actually are. Requires long-term investment and often major life decisions/changes.

Lifestyle — A blanket term for the quality and types of activities, interests and people one spends the majority of their time with. Your profession, the place you live, hobbies, friends, and weekend trips are all components of your overall lifestyle. Your lifestyle is a reflection of your values and self-esteem and also determines your demographics. A lifestyle can be based upon unconfident behavior (i.e., dressing a certain way or driving a certain car in order to impress women). *See Also: Demographics*

Limiting Beliefs — Irrational beliefs that inherently prevent one from being successful at something. Limiting beliefs are almost always untrue and results of defense mechanisms and a lack of courage. An example is a man who believes that women will never be attracted to him because he's bald so he doesn't even try. *See Also: Defense Mechanisms, Courage*

Narcissism - Men who overcompensate for their low self-esteem and lack of confidence by imposing their will and needs onto others unnecessarily. Narcissism is often preoccupied with sleeping with as many women as possible. Narcissistic behavior is often promoted within the Pick Up Artist industry and the so-called "red pill" community. Narcissistic behavior can come across as confident but is still low-status behavior because it is over-invested in the perceptions of others. Men who are narcissistic experience short-term sexual success but long-term emotional failure. *See Also: Self-Esteem, Non-Neediness, Pick Up Artist*

Neediness — Being more invested in the opinions and perceptions of others than your opinion and perception of yourself. Needy men end up deferring all decision-making and behaviors to what they will believe will win them approval from others. They will subvert their own identity and desires for the will of others. Neediness is a defense mechanism for social/emotional failures early in life but is a failing strategy for intimacy in adulthood. Neediness is overcome through investing in oneself, practicing vulnerability, and pursuing Honest Living, Honest Action, and Honest Communication.

Non-neediness — Being more invested in your opinion of yourself than the opinions others have of you. Non-neediness is one component of having high self-esteem and the root of all attractive behavior. True Confidence is achieved through practicing vulnerability and in investing in oneself. *See Also: Confidence, Neediness, Self-Esteem*

Objectification — The decision to view women and social interactions as impersonal processes and objects rather than people and emotional activities. Seeing women as numbers, subjects to be studied, games to be won, etc., are all common ways which men objectify their sexual and emotional lives. Emotions are ignored and discouraged from being expressed. Narcissism and Performance behaviors both encourage objectification in order to achieve short-term success. Objectification causes long-term emotional damage and can lead to depression and even lower levels of self-esteem. This is the reason for the paradoxical situation many long-time narcissistic men find themselves in: they have many sexual partners but find themselves to actually be *less* happy than they were when they started. *See Also: Narcissism, Pick Up Artists*

Pain Period — The period of time when one begins to open themselves up emotionally and make themselves more vulnerable to others. This temporarily causes one to behave in a less attractive manner as they sort through years of emotional baggage and trauma. It's usually a period accompanied by a lot of emotional stress and pain. The pain period is necessary to go from a low self-esteem and unconfident person to a high self-esteem and True Confidence person. *See Also: Vulnerability, Non-neediness*

Pick Up Artist — A school of dating advice based on the teachings of Erik von Markovik (Mystery) and Neil Strauss (Style), as well as Real Social Dynamics. Pick Up Artists are characterized by their own specific lingo and measurement for success, which is getting laid as much as possible. Pick Up Artists objectify their emotional and sexual lives and, therefore, cause long-term psychological damage to themselves despite often having sex with women . Many Pick Up Artist teachings encourage Narcissism and performance-based behavior. *See Also: Narcissism, Performance, Objectification*

Polarization — Behavior that forces a woman to feel strongly about you, whether positive or negative. Polarization is useful for screening out women who are most compatible with you very quickly. Polarization not only invites rejection but uses it as a tool to achieve dating success efficiently. *See Also: Assortment Effect, Demographics, Rejection*

Projection — A common defense mechanism used by both men and women to avoid anxiety. Projection is when you perceive the source of your anxiety to have the insecurity rather than yourself. For instance, an Indian man who is insecure about his race will project onto the women he meets that they are racist and don't like him because he's Indian. A man who is insecure about women being mean to him will project onto women who intimidate him that they are bitches and use that as a reason to avoid them. Women project as well. As a man, it is possible to be rejected a woman who is very attracted to you because she's insecure or uncomfortable with her sexuality. For instance, if a woman is low self-esteem and perceives you to be too attractive for her, she will project onto you that insecurity and get mad at you for only wanting her for sex. This is the reason why less attractive women may reject you more often and harsher than more attractive women. *See Also: Defense Mechanisms*

Rejection — When a woman demonstrates a lack of interest in a man's sexual intent. Rejection can be overt (i.e., "I have a boyfriend, sorry,") or subtle (i.e., flaking, going to the bathroom and not coming back, etc.).

Seduction - The process in which a man induces a woman to become more highly invested in him than he is in her. Sex is a side effect of this process. Women are generally always less invested at the beginning of an interaction because they almost always have more sexual and romantic options than men do.

Self-Esteem — One's unconscious perception of their own value or self-worth. Confidence in sexual interactions is one component of having high self-esteem. For the sake of clarity, this book uses the term "non-neediness" in place of self-esteem in most cases to express the relational component of self-esteem. *See Also: Non-Neediness, Attractive Behavior, Finding Your Truth*

Self-Selection — The unconscious process of the assortment effect. Self-Selection is the idea that no matter what you do or who you are, you are going to be attractive to one particular demographic and unattractive to others. For instance, if you're tall and bald, you're going to unconsciously screen for women who like tall, bald men for no other reason than women who don't will reject you or display no interest in you. If you're a foreigner, then you will automatically self-select for women who are interested in foreigners without having to do anything. Similar to the assortment effect, but instead of reflecting beliefs and attitudes, self-selection reflects superficial preferences. *See Also: Assortment Effect, Demographics*

Sexual Anxiety — When one experiences apprehension and fear when expressing their sexuality or when confronted with sexual situations. *See Also: Courage, Defense Mechanisms*

Sexual Escalation — The process in which two people become more and more sexually engaged. Typically follows a pattern of light touching, to holding and heavy touching, to kissing, then foreplay and eventually sex.

Sexual Intent — An expressed desire to have sexual relations with someone. Can be overt and obvious or subtle and implied through flirting. *See Also: Creepy, Flirting*

Social Anxiety — When one experiences fear and apprehension in social situations or when meeting new people. *See Also: Courage, Defense Mechanisms*

Social Circle — A group of mutual friends and acquaintances.

Social Proof — The psychological mechanism where if many other people value something, then we will value it as well. In attraction, the theory goes that if a number of other people or women are attracted to you, then one specific woman will become more attracted to you. Only applicable in social circle situations. For instance, if you walk into a bar and a number of women show interest in you, then a woman on the other side of the bar who shares no mutual acquaintances is not going to care. But if you walk into a bar and three of a woman's female friends know you and like you, then she is likely to be attracted to you before you even speak to her.

Unconditionality — Performing an action or saying something with no expectations of receiving anything in return. Men often do attractive behaviors or nice things with the expectation that the girl now owes them something in return. A common example is he will compliment her with the expectation that she's supposed to be nice to him in return. This is conditional behavior. Conditional behavior is unconfident and generally backfires and makes one appear less attractive. Unconditional behavior is an action with no expectations for anything in return. Unconditionality is confident and therefore attractive.

Vulnerability — Being unguarded or undefended in expressing one's thoughts and emotions. Most men hide the thoughts and emotions they believe will make them less attractive. This forces them to behave conditionally and base their behaviors on the beliefs and perceptions of those around them. This is unconfident behavior and ultimately makes them unattractive. Paradoxically, making oneself vulnerable and surrendering to criticism and not expecting anything in return from others causes one to build self-esteem, become more confident and more attractive.

Further Reading

If you feel you gained a lot from this book and have never read my website, then that is the next logical destination. It's www.markmanson.net and is regularly updated with articles, musings and stories.

Recommended Reading:

No More Mr. Nice Guy by Robert Glover — the definitive book on helping men break out of habits of neediness and ending "Nice Guy" behavior that sabotages their relationships.

How to Win Friends and Influence People by Dale Carnegie — A classic on basic social skills and making good impressions on others.

Getting the Love You Want by Harville Hendrix – Cheesy title but indispensable book on relationships, emotional baggage, and why we become attracted to who we're attracted to.

Attached by Amir Levine and Rachel Heller – A primer on attachment theory, why we become so insecure in intimacy and attraction and steps on overcoming that insecurity.

The Evolution of Desire by David Buss — A good scientific overview of sex studies and biological differences in male and female sexuality.

The Definitive Book of Body Language by Allan and Barbara Pease — A must-read for anyone who has trouble deciphering people's emotions through body language.

About the Author

Mark Manson is from Austin, Texas, USA and graduated from Boston University in 2007. He began coaching men informally that same year, taking them out to local bars and helping them approach attractive women.

Soon after, Mark founded a dating consultancy business for men and worked as a full-time dating consultant from 2008 until 2012. *Models: Attract Women Through Honesty* was first self-published in 2011. It was then revised in 2012 and again in 2016.

In 2013, Mark moved away from consulting and dating advice and now writes on a wide range of topics for both genders. You can discover more of his writing at www.markmanson.net.

Mark is now married and currently lives in New York City.